51 QUESTIONS
ON SOCIAL
ENTREPRENEURSHIP

BY NEETAL PAREKH

Quad Press
An imprint of Innovate Impact Media
211 Hope Street, #391773
Mountain View, CA 94039

Revised Edition

Interior illustrations by verynice design studio
Cover design inspired by Dominika Peschak
Interior book design by Sue Balcer, JustYourTypeDTP

Learn more on Innov8social
www.innov8social.com

Library of Congress Control Number: 2015920062
ISBN: 978-0-9907482-0-5

*Dedicated to our greater selves; who think big, love more,
live without fear, and dare the impossible.*

Foreword

by John Montgomery

This is the most exciting time to be alive and in business because the collective consciousness of humanity is on the rise, shifting to being altruistic and global from being selfish, tribal and local. In business, this shift is reflected in a re-orientation to a triple bottom line approach—planet, people, profit—from a solitary focus on profits. Social entrepreneurs and their businesses are leading this shift.

Social entrepreneurship is a reflection of this evolution of consciousness. At its core is the disruptive innovation that successful businesses not only must create a profit but also have a material positive effect on society and the environment. Social entrepreneurship is better suited than conventional business to help our one human family take better care of each other and our shared planetary home.

As consciousness evolves, corporations that exist to optimize both social good and profit replace corporations that exist solely to maximize profits for shareholders. In the new paradigm, corporations compete to not only be the best in the world but also to be the best for the world. The vehicles for this new paradigm are new corporate forms such as the benefit corporation, which are structurally aligned with the foundational premise of social entrepreneurship because they expressly authorize the simultaneous pursuit of profit and social impact.

The benefit corporation is also a disruptive innovation because it contains legal architecture to support a social and environmental conscience that transcends and includes the usual pecuniary, profit-oriented one. It is the first significant innovation in corporate law since 1811 when New York combined free incorporation and limited liability. These innovations quickly became standard features in corporations around the world and enabled the liability-free flow of investment capital that fueled the Age of Industry. Social enterprises incorporated as benefit corporations herald the start of Age of Interdependence in which business is conducted as if people and place matter.

Silicon Valley has unleashed many disruptive innovations—the personal computer, the cell phone, the browser to name a few—which spread rapidly to become the global standard. Adoption is slow at first with mass adoption coming only after a tipping point where a sufficient number of pioneers and early adopters have shown that the new technology is safe for the masses. Once it has taken hold, however, we wonder how we possibly could have existed without it.

Social entrepreneurship approaches its tipping point where doing business this way is the norm. In less than 10 years, most businesses in the world will be social enterprises pursuing profit as well as positive social impact. Business schools will train MBA students to think with a social impact mindset. Social impact will be reflected in new accounting systems such as those being developed by the Sustainability Accounting Standards Board (SASB) and in public company disclosures. We will look back and wonder how we could possibly done business any other way.

Now, however, there is still resistance to social entrepreneurship because it is relatively new. Happily, this approach is a better way to do business. The preliminary economic data indicates that corporations built for the new paradigm[1] with

---

1 See, for example: The Impact of a Corporate Culture of Sustainability on Corporate Behavior and Performance, Eccles et al, Harvard Business School Working Paper, November 2011 and From the Stockholder to the Stakeholder: How Sustainability Can Drive Financial Outperformance, University of Oxford and Arabesque Partners, March 2015

cultures of sustainability out-perform their conventional peers. This book does a great service to the new paradigm by taking the fear out of social entrepreneurship and inspiring its readers to join in the great adventure of co-creating a more humane and sustainable global economic system.

51 Questions on Social Entrepreneurship will help social entrepreneurship reach its tipping point more quickly. This book makes a significant contribution to accelerating the global shift in consciousness by de-mystifying social entrepreneurship and making it intelligible and accessible not only to aspiring social entrepreneurs but also to anyone interested in learning about the topic, including venture capitalists, attorneys, management consultants, accountants and investors.

The author, Neetal Parekh, tackles the most frequently asked questions about social entrepreneurship in a straightforward and creative manner. Unlike most business books, which are written in the tiresome voice of an omniscient narrator, this book answers the questions by taking the reader on a journey through the voices of three fictional social entrepreneurs who develop a successful social enterprise. At journey's end, you will not only understand social entrepreneurship but also will be inspired and empowered to create your own successful social enterprise.

* * *

John Montgomery[2] is a corporate attorney in Silicon Valley and founder and Chairman Emeritus of Montgomery & Hansen LLP. He co-chaired the committee to draft benefit corporation legislation in California, is the Chairman of Startworks Ventures—a benefit capital firm—and author of *Great from the Start: How Conscious Corporations Attract Success.*

2 For more, see interview with John Montgomery http://www.innov8social.com/2015/09/interview-with-john-montgomery-social-enterprise-attorney

TABLE OF CONTENTS

Introduction

I AM SO EXCITED to share this book with you! It is the product of years of exploring fascinating concepts of social entrepreneurship through education, life, work experiences, and through launching innov8social.com. Though it took longer than expected (as everyone said it would), I am thrilled to be able to hand over this part of me to you.

WHO SHOULD READ THE BOOK?

This book is for:

- **Startup founders and co-founders** seeking to create social impact with their ventures.

- **Aspiring entrepreneurs and innovators** and those considering starting a social impact venture in the future.

- **Professionals** who want to understand more about the field of social innovation, social entrepreneurship, and social enterprise.

- **Students** at all levels who are looking for a multi-lens view into the social impact venture space.

- **Companies and intrapreneurs** seeking to better understand the growing social impact sector to incorporate into their businesses and careers.

- **Informed consumers** who realize that we vote with every dollar we spend.

- **Anyone who wants to explore social impact**.

- **Anyone who likes a story.** And if you enjoy reading through listening as much as I do, you may also enjoy the audiobook version as well. :)

WHAT MAKES THE BOOK INTERESTING, RELEVANT, AND FUN?

The book is meant to be an accessible, actionable, and friendly introduction to topics related to social innovation and social entrepreneurship. To help make it easier to follow, these features have been incorporated:

- **It is a Q&A of 51 questions** that can be read in order or piecemeal to make it easy to find what you are looking for in whichever stage of learning and research you are in.

- **It is composed in a story format,** featuring a host of characters (not real) and their quest for actionable information (totally real) for their own idea, making the process of reading fun and engaging! The story also puts common social entrepreneurship questions into context, so you know how they could apply to you and your social impact journey . The characters help frame different perspectives and connect you to what drives their work.

- **It points to other resources so you can further your exploration.** Ebook readers can click on resources to directly and easily reach live links. Where relevant, I have linked to updateable posts on Innov8social.com so you can engage through comments and even suggest additions and edits.

- **The questions are based on some of the most popular blog posts on Innov8social.com,** so you know you are getting answers to questions that other readers and online users are searching for as well.

WHAT DOES THE BOOK COVER?

The book is set up with three main characters and aspiring co-founders: Sara, Jay, and Tino. We join them as they explore the prospect of starting a social enterprise—a business that embodies their guiding desire to create impact as well as make a profit.

Of course, they have a lot of questions. We will tag along as they talk to various individuals and with each other on topics including:

- Definitions for terms like social entrepreneurship, social innovation, social enterprise, and social business

- Whether they should try to be a social enterprise, and the benefits and drawbacks of the designation

- New and emerging legal forms for social enterprises

- How social enterprises raise funds

- The complexities and necessities of measuring impact

- How they can deepen their knowledge of social entrepreneurship through outside resources

- How they can support other social entrepreneurs and social enterprises

WHAT WILL I KNOW AFTER READING THE BOOK?

You will understand the social enterprise landscape and learn actionable information to help you make decisions on furthering your social impact ideas and your potential to create social impact in your daily life.

You will also learn how Sara, Jay, and Tino fare in their adventure in social entrepreneurship.

Now, let's get started with the first question, addressing the essential question driving this book, the "why." Whenever exploring a new topic, and maybe it's the skeptic in me, but I always like to ask—what's the point? Why does this matter? It's only because I have found the *why* behind social impact and social entrepreneurship so compelling that I have dedicated my efforts to projects like this book.

1 WHAT'S THE POINT—WHY DOES SOCIAL IMPACT EVEN MATTER?

The world is changing, and everywhere we look there seems to be a call to action.

On the horizon, we can see a world population that will reach eight billion people in the next decade—double what it was just fifty years prior. Climate change, which has been recognized as a global concern by institutions ranging from the EPA to the Papacy, threatens with extreme weather patterns as well as a rise in sea level and impact on existing species. Wealth inequity has a new definition as half of the world's wealth is now owned by less than 1% of the global population, and we live in a time in which nearly 3 billion people struggle to survive on less than $2 a day and nearly 1 billion people don't have enough food to eat. We live in a time in which girls globally are not afforded the same access to education, with 33 million fewer girls than boys attending middle school around the world.

Fortunately, the story doesn't end here.

We also live in a moment when we have ready problem solvers and incredible advances in technology that let us imagine impact not in magnitudes of hundreds of lives improved, but in magnitudes of billions. We are in a moment in which our workforce is changing, and so are their values.

2015 marked the first time that millennials comprised a majority of the workforce and the first time generation Z began their significant entry into the workforce. By 2025, millennials will make up 75% and Gen Z over 20% of our working economy. That matters because when asked, the vast majority of millennials express their desire to use their skills for good, and Gen Z-ers, having grown up in times of financial and political instability, seek to make the world significantly better. These generations, more than any preceding them, have prioritized creating impact in their equations for a life well-lived.

This ethos doesn't just impact the workforce, but also informs how and what individuals buy and the kinds of companies they launch and scale.

As of the end of 2015, over 30 states or jurisdictions in the US have passed some form of social enterprise legal structure, with nearly 3,000 companies choosing to adopt these new legal structures. Additionally, companies including Rally Software and Etsy that have aligned with the social enterprise movement through pursuing a "B corporation" certification have had an Initial Public Offering (IPO). Others, such as Laureate Education, have chosen to convert to a benefit corporation and also file an IPO.[1]

As we stand at the edge of how things have always been done and how they can be done, we can see divergent but complementary forces: the pressing issues that affect our generation and most definitely will affect future generations and the intelligent, engaged, motivated army of problem solvers ready to do something about it.

While the evolution of social entrepreneurship to this point has seen the carving out of a new kind of business and a vocabulary to define terms in this emerging space, the urgent need

---

1 http://lawprofessors.typepad.com/business_law/2015/10/laureate-education-first-ipo-for-a-benefit-corporation.html

for leadership and innovation has the potential to be met by the most driven, largest, and most cross-functional social innovators and social entrepreneurs the world has ever known.

There is the potential to work beyond subsects of entrepreneurship and focus on redefining the future of business as a whole and to consider impact as a norm. There is the possibility of broadening the reach of social entrepreneurship by absorbing its core attributes into the character of business itself. Instead of being "social entrepreneurship," the values of measuring, reporting, and expanding impact could become part of the way we understand, assess, and measure the success of industries across the board—making it part of "business as usual."

This massive potential—this meeting of what we need and what we are capable of giving, of limitless possibility and urgent problems, of compounding concerns and creative and committed problem solvers—to me encapsulates the essence of why social entrepreneurship matters. I have no doubt that it has the ability to not only transform our lives individually, but to collectively change the world.

CHAPTER 1

Meet Sara, Jay, and Tino— Aspiring Entrepreneurs

SARA

The gen Z student entrepreneur

SARA, BORN IN THE LATE 1990s, is part of the growing group of emerging students and professionals known as "Generation Z."

She embodies the values and mindset attributed to her generation—she is a digital native—born after the advent of mobile phones and social media and is incredibly tech-savvy; she prefers texting over calling, is eager to use her skills for good, feels the most productive when she is collaborating, and loves her independence and autonomy.

She identifies with newer millennials and contemporaries of her gen Z cohort because experiencing the "Great Recession" in middle school literally shifted her path on everything from college to contemplating her career. Sara's family was personally impacted as her father lost his job after his company downsized, and her mother's hours were reduced at her part-time position. They had to sell their home and move out of their neighborhood. It took nearly half of a decade for their lives to get back to "normal" or a new normal with her parents in good jobs and their family living without a recurring fear of a repeat. Sara spent a lot of her high school years worrying about her family's financial stability and feeling like the systems and economics that were supposed to protect and support families like hers had somehow failed them.

Sara grew up in Kansas and after high school decided to save money and go to a local community college. It gave her the chance to take on a job and pay for her education. She graduated with dual associates degrees in business and nutrition about a year ago. She, like a number of her classmates, has taken multiple online classes from top universities around the country, often for free or a nominal cost. In Sara's case, she enrolled in a handful of courses to better understand the intersection of food, sociology, and business.

Sara, also like many of her peers, is passionate about creating impact with her life and work.

She has been particularly moved by issues around food— especially creating access to good nutrition. She first began to understand the need for making healthy food more accessible through her trips to rural parts of the state with her family. During the recession, people who hadn't experienced food shortages before were figuring out how to make ends meet and feed their families. Her family would drive to food banks and volunteer with the sorting and delivering of boxes of mixed food items.

After graduation and with savings from her various jobs, Sara made the bold move to pack up her bags and get on a plane to Oakland, California. She was ready to take her knowledge and experience to the next level and work with others passionate about food issues.

It took a few months to get settled in, but Sara now works at a local co-op and volunteers regularly at Second Harvest, a large food bank that collects, sorts, and distributes food to communities in need. She dreams about creating a business that solves a problem in the food and nutrition space and has met a number of passionate community leaders and startup companies who are similarly motivated.

Sara intends to finish her college degree and considers this her "gap" year or two to gain valuable work and life experience and save up for college. She is beyond excited about the prospect of becoming an entrepreneur and creating impact with her work.

JAY

The millennial law student

Jay is the first in his family to go to law school and is also a first-generation American.

Back in India, where his parents were born and where he lived until he was three, most of his relatives owned their own small businesses. His great-grandfather had been in the textile trade, shipping textiles from India to the British Empire and Asia.

Jay was born in Bhuj, a rural village in central India, and his family took a leap of faith and moved to Washington, D.C. when he was a toddler and his sister was just a few years older. His dad owned a small retail store, and Jay grew up watching his parents juggle the challenges and opportunities of being both first-generation Americans and entrepreneurs.

2001 marked a number of shifts for his family and their

realities. Early in the year, a major earthquake struck near where he grew up in Bhuj. Jay was in high school at the time, and he and his mother went back that summer to help. He was startled to see how much it had devastated the entire area. He volunteered with a non-government organization (an "NGO," also called a nonprofit) to build new homes and helped his extended family and their neighbors move into the new housing before coming back to the US.

Then, in September, soon after they returned from the summer in India, 9/11 changed everything. The fall of the Twin Towers of the World Trade Center in New York City, the plane striking the Pentagon, and the other grounded outside of D.C. created deep sadness in humanity and new tensions at school and for his father's business. Though there was a unifying sense of resilience and strength that arose after 9/11, there was also danger for immigrant communities like Jay's family. Their small shop was vandalized with racial epithets sprayed across the door. Jay was held at gunpoint one night when closing the store. "Live through it, find ways to heal, and rebuild" became Jay's personal mantra.

His family made the challenging decision to sell the business and pursue another outside of the city. The decade after involved considerable adjustment, but they found peace and solitude in their decision and also worked with local communities to foster interfaith and racial tolerance.

After high school, Jay started his journey westward, finishing college in Chicago. He had majored in economics and business, but the desire to engage more deeply in something directly impactful weighed on him. He took a bold step by not taking a full-time position after college, and decided instead to dedicate the next year to AmeriCorps—which took him further west.

AmeriCorps is a government-supported intensive one-year service program. Jay was assigned to work at a civic organization in downtown San Francisco focusing on issues affecting urban youth. The work led him not only to counsel numerous at-risk youth and understand their daily challenges but also to see the various laws and policies the organization supported to improve access to education and healthcare for the population they served.

Jay made his second bold step, this time to pursue law school. He shadowed the pro bono attorney who supported the organization and felt hopeful that he could create a new path by going into law. He took the LSAT a few times before getting a score that could win him a spot at one of the well-regarded local law schools.

Now, he is in his second year of law school in the greater San Francisco Bay area. He is eager to find ways to combine his love of legal systems with his passion for social impact. Having been surrounded by entrepreneurs growing up, he is also excited about exploring the intersection of law, business, and social impact.

TINO

The seasoned serial entrepreneur

Tino is a lifelong entrepreneur and, most recently, a new grandfather.

He was born in Guatemala in the late 1940s during the Guatemalan Revolution. It was a decade of unique social reform for the country, including literacy programs and democratic participation. His parents, both professors outside of Guatemala City, would always tell him about the shift in consciousness they witnessed during this time.

Tino has vague memories of the Revolution, but most of his childhood and youth was during the three-decades-long civil war within the country from the 1960s to well into the 1990s. He counts the political and economic instability as one of the primary catalysts to his early foray into entrepreneurship.

Tino started his first modestly successful business selling

books door-to-door at the age of ten. By the time he was in his late teens, he was running a highly profitable business managing a small team of contractors and handymen to do repairs in local homes and businesses. His parents encouraged his entrepreneurial tendencies but pressed him on his studies.

So when he received a scholarship to attend an engineering program in Idaho, he couldn't refuse the offer. It was a major move to transition from a massive city in Guatemala and a civil war to a sleepy college town in Pacific Northwest USA. He embraced the opportunity and excelled in engineering, economics, and global development studies.

He felt an urgency and drive to realize the "American Dream" and achieve incredible success in his career. The engineering degree led him to work for a startup company in San Jose—the heart of entrepreneurial "Silicon Valley" and he has remained in the area for the better part of thirty years.

Soon after his first few jobs in increasingly large companies, he swapped out his engineer's hat for an entrepreneur's one. Tino has started all kinds of businesses ranging from ventures in hardware to mobile technology and, most recently, in virtual currencies like Bitcoin.

He has experienced flat-out failures—including the time he had to file for bankruptcy after a particularly challenging startup nosedived—along with incredible success—including the acquisition of one of his companies by Google. Tino has served on the boards of a few nonprofit organizations but has never been part of a business focused on social impact.

For all intents and purposes, he achieved a version of that American Dream he rallied for. He built businesses of which he was both proud and which allowed him the means to raise a family and provide good-paying jobs to countless employees and contractors. He always imagined bringing his siblings to California or planning a massive reunion for his parents and family. Life had gotten so busy that he figured he would focus on the reunion when things eased up a bit. But then in 2008 he received word that his youngest sister had developed an unexpected and serious brain hemorrhage. By the time he boarded a plane and reached his family, his little sister had already passed away.

The sad event was devastating for his family and for him personally. He felt a need to step away from the intensity of running multiple businesses and instead engage in work that would be part of his legacy.

So, Tino took a bold step with the support of his family. After applying a few years back, Tino and his wife accepted the joint opportunity to serve as Peace Corps fellows in Botswana. There, they worked on economic development and food projects with local communities. It opened Tino's eyes to the need for new ways of doing business.

Though he considers himself a no-frills pragmatist, he sees a compelling case for companies thinking about impact *now*, when it can do the most for future generations, including his grandkids. After his time in Botswana, he is back in the US and ready to immerse himself in a new venture—one that prioritizes impact as well as profit.

How They Meet: IMPACTATHON San Francisco

Sara, Jay, and Tino meet at *IMPACTATHON SF*, a five-day, immersive hackathon-style workshop in San Francisco designed for aspiring entrepreneurs seeking to create impact.

The event they are participating in, IMPACTATHON, features a five-day hackathon for social impact startups and social entrepreneurs with various modules of instruction and support and guidance from organizers. It runs Monday through Friday and culminates in a formal pitch to an audience of peers, supporters, community members, potential investors and partners, as well as a panel of judges.

"Hackathon" workshops like this one force creative thinking and quick prototyping because of the time constraint and because each team has to pitch their startup idea to an audience of potential investors and advisors.

Top pitches, as voted by the judging panel and audience, can receive free office space, complimentary access to helpful software and web tools, admission into accelerator programs to help take their ideas to the next stage, and even funding. A lot can happen in a few days for aspiring entrepreneurs! As with many such immersive hackathon events, past participants who speak to the crowd underscore that individuals and teams will get out of the experience what they put into it.

At IMPACTATHON, participants have the option of giving a brief, initial outline of their social impact startup ideas to attract potential teammates and co-founders. Then all of the attendees mingle and "vote" informally on top ideas. In this way, ideas that resonate or have traction tend to gain support and team members.

MONDAY AT IMPACTATHON

Sara lines up behind other workshop participants waiting to make their initial pitch. She is thinking of ways to clearly express an idea that can combine nutrition and social impact in a meaningful way, and that might attract a few others to join her. What if she gets nervous and doesn't express herself well? What if no one is interested? She hasn't articulated the idea in front of a group and is much more interested in finding a great team motivated by a similar mission than in actualizing the specific idea she has. Before she knows it, it's her turn.

"Hi, I'm Sara. I'm passionate about nutrition and impact.

My idea is to create a business that delivers fresh food to areas where there aren't supermarkets, farmer's markets, local grocery stores, or other sources of healthy food. I think we can create a business that helps solve the problem of lack of access to good nutrition and one that people will love to buy from. If you're interested, come by; I would love to talk to you!"

* * *

After a few dozen initial pitches, IMPACTATHON participants mingle, and those who pitched carry neon yellow index cards with their idea name. Attendees walk around, ask more questions, and "vote" for initial ideas they like by taping a paper straw to the index card. People tend to vote for ideas they like, that they wish were already reality, and sometimes to support their friends or existing team.

Sara is grateful for the chance to share her idea and gauge any interest. It's something she has been thinking about for some time. It aligns with everything she is interested in: being part of a startup team, working on food issues, and creating both profit and impact with her work. She is also particularly interested in finding out more about what it means for a business to be for-profit, seeking investment as well as pursuing impact. She is interested in building out the line of products and services they will deliver that support the overall intent to deliver fresh, healthy food to those lacking access.

With so many ideas and participants, there is a buzz around certain ideas. The app that will let people report overuse of water by residents and businesses has at least ten votes and a line of participants waiting to talk to the founder. Another idea about using drones to help find missing children is also popular among the crowd. It doesn't hurt that the founder of that idea actually brought her own drone!

Sara's idea isn't one of the top, and a few people walk by and congratulate her on her idea and presentation but apologize that they have already used all of their votes. She gets a couple of straws taped to her card, but the voters seem drawn to actually commit their time to other teams.

Then, Jay walks over. He votes for Sara's idea and another one focusing on creating a smartphone app to make it easier for people to get informed on new policy or legislation proposals in their counties and cities. He ultimately chooses Sara's idea because he relates with her enthusiasm and passion, and he thinks her idea will have a more practical business model.

He is also excited to hear Sara's focus on building a company that has a social motivation in addition to profit. He suggests that they think beyond a strong corporate social responsibility (CSR) to form a company in which impact is really core to its formation. He shares his experience at a few legal seminars in the previous semester and about unique, new legal structures for companies dedicated to a particular mission or impact objective. He doesn't know much about them yet but is eager to find out more and possibly become part of forming one.

Tino, who was invited to mentor groups, decides to jump in and participate in the voting after hearing the initial pitches. Though he is a seasoned entrepreneur, he hasn't worked on a mission-driven venture. He initially votes for two other ideas related to creating social impact through implementing wearable devices or mobile technology, but ultimately approaches Sara because he finds the problem she is trying to solve simple and straightforward and the solution unique and interesting.

As a serial entrepreneur and occasional investor, Tino approaches this startup idea as he does every other one he has co-founded—from a practical and decisive perspective. He needs to know that the numbers will make sense and that the business case is sound. He knows the market for fresh food in certain areas is substantial and growing. In fact, he has learned that the overall market for grocery buyers who consciously purchase healthier, more sustainable food is in the hundreds of billions of dollars.[2] And it's growing rapidly. To Tino, it makes good sense to create a business around a product and service that will not only deliver something people want and are willing to pay for, but that also has the potential to improve the health and well-being of customers.

Besides, Tino has a bit of experience in this because he worked on a pretty complex food delivery project during his time in Botswana. He thinks a company like this has the potential not only to be sustainable, but to also turn a profit in the long run— all by giving people the means to live healthier lives. If the idea goes beyond these few days at the workshop, he would even be willing to invest his own funds in the company.

* * *

They introduce themselves a bit more to each other and talk about how they can work as a small team to tackle a number of demanding tasks over the next few days, their goals for the final presentation, and what roles each can play in crafting a compelling (and hopefully, winning) pitch. Sara is thrilled to have Jay and Tino's interest and expertise to help make this idea happen.

So, they start.

They decide to break down the remaining time based on elements of storytelling and pitching that were presented in the Pitching 101 session of the workshop. The organizers mention Guy Kawasaki's "10 Slide Pitch Deck" as a good sample set of slides for preparing a pitch to any audience, especially investors, as detailed in his book *Art of the Start 2.0*.[3]

---

2 Lifestyles of Health and Sustainability (LOHAS). Retrieved from http://lohas.groupsite.com/main/summary
3 "The Only 10 Slides You Need in a Pitch Deck". Kawaski, Guy. Retrieved from http://guykawasaki.com/the-only-10-slides-you-need-in-your-pitch/

Sara, Tino, and Jay work in a team and refine the idea for delivering healthy, fresh food to underserved urban youth and their families where local, fresh options are hard to come by. They know the idea might change or pivot along the way, but after discussing options in depth, they feel on the same page about the core aspects of the business.

Slide 1: Title—Deciding on a Name

They begin brainstorming a name. They think about how they can capture the positive feeling of nutritious food along with the convenience of delivery. After creating a list of over fifty possible names, Tino suggests looking at what domain names are available in case they want to create a website.

In the end, it makes sense to combine a few words that help convey their idea, and they land on the name *FreshDashDeliver*.[4]

Slide 2: Defining a Problem—a Closer Look at "Food Deserts"

They start with defining the problem and opportunity.

From their initial research, Sara, Jay, and Tino discover that there is actually a name for areas where access to fresh food is limited. The US Department of Agriculture (USDA) defined the term "food desert" specifically to describe areas such "as urban neighborhoods and rural towns without ready access to fresh, healthy, and affordable food. Instead of supermarkets and grocery stores, these communities may have no food access or are served only by fast food restaurants and convenience stores that offer few healthy, affordable food options."[5]

---

4 freshdashdeliver.com
5 USDA.gov. Retrieved from http://apps.ams.usda.gov/fooddeserts/fooddeserts.aspx

Relevant to defining the problem and opportunity, they discover:

- Food deserts are not isolated occurrences—because an estimated 23.5 million people in the US live in food deserts, and more than half are low-income individuals.[6]

- Studies suggest individuals living in food deserts are twice as likely to pass away from diabetes than those who have ready access to healthy foods.[7]

- Though food deserts can be found in rural areas, they are a big part of big cities too. For example, in Chicago nearly one million people live in food deserts or areas with more fast-food chains than grocery stores. Similarly, New York, Los Angeles,[8] Oakland, New Orleans, and Baltimore[9]—where one in four people are said to lack easy access to healthy food—are also sites of food deserts or lack easy access to healthy food.

- The White House issued a goal of eliminating food deserts by 2017 and allocated $400 million to solutions, mostly in the form of tax breaks to supermarkets.[10]

Slide 3: Defining a Solution and Value Proposition— Deciding What to Build Together

As part of the workshop, they have to not only come up with an idea but also build a basic prototype—at least enough to get feedback from potential users. This will help them to define a "value proposition," i.e., defining the value their solution

---

6 USDA.gov. Retrieved from http://apps.ams.usda.gov/fooddeserts/fooddeserts.aspx
7 Food Empowerment Project. Retrieved from http://www.foodispower.org/food-deserts/
8 Food Empowerment Project. Retrieved from http://www.foodispower.org/food-deserts/
9 "1 in 4 Baltimore Residents Live in a Food Desert". Retrieved from http://www.jhsph.edu/research/centers-and-in-stitutes/johns-hopkins-center-for-a-livable-future/news-room/News-Releases/2015/1-In-4-Baltimore-Residents-Live-Food-Desert.html
10 "11 Facts About Food Deserts" [DoSomething.org]. Retrieved from https://www.dosomething.org/facts/11-facts-about-food-deserts

will deliver to its customers. A value proposition helps nail down how a company proposes to solve a particular customer problem.

Since they are early in the process and have not built or tested a solution, Tino suggests keeping the value proposition fairly broad. He makes a few suggestions and they tumble the phrasing until they get to one they like.

"*FreshDashDeliver* delivers fresh, healthy food to underserved neighborhoods and families."

Slide 4: What Makes Them Unique

The next slide is supposed to show what will make them unique. This could include a compelling design, intuitive user experience, or unique algorithms or data analysis that will give their solution an edge or even an "unfair advantage."

Ideally, they should have a basic prototype ready. That way everyone from potential users to the judges can see and potentially even interact with or try the solution.

This is hard.

They spend a number of hours on the first day on this element. Could the mode of transportation they choose differentiate them? They were thinking trucks, but maybe they could use less costly modes such as bicycles or motorized scooters. If they do pursue delivery by truck, maybe they could create an app that could more efficiently map out routes for delivering food without wasting time, fuel, or resources.

As they think through these critical elements, Jay brings up a few points.

> *Jay:* "You know, we don't really know much about social impact companies. We don't know how they work or don't work, and I don't know about you guys—but a lot the

terms sound the same to me. I've heard social entrepreneurship, social innovation, social enterprise.... We have a lot to do, but do you think we should split forces and try to learn more? It could help us figure out our distinguishing features."

Sara: "Yes, to everything! I have really been wanting to know about this. I actually have a family friend who is kind of an expert in this space. I was just reading a magazine article she wrote about companies that are committed to social impact. I could see if she is in town and meet up with her tomorrow morning if she's free."

Tino: "Do it. We're at the right time to think big, because as we get closer we're going to be in total crunch time. After tonight we will have four full days and then the final presentation. Honestly, it's not an end-all, be-all to win or place here. I mean, we can still definitely pursue this idea if we don't. But from my experience, these little opportunities to get recognized and validated or win free stuff like office space, etc. can be helpful in building relationships down the road.

"Jay, you also mentioned being interested in legal structures. Do you think you can find out more about that by tomorrow too? I have a friend who has a fund that I think exclusively works with mission-driven companies. I'll see if I can meet her too."

Sara: "Ok, awesome! Let's work on asking these questions and then catch each other up on what we learn."

They wrap up the first night well after sunset, the adrenaline from the day making it hard to let go.

CHAPTER 2

What is Social Entrepreneurship?

TUESDAY AT IMPACTATHON

SARA CALLS A FAMILY FRIEND, Shonda, as she's leaving the workshop.

Shonda has led or started half a dozen companies in the past three decades. While her parents were born outside of Kingston, Jamaica, she was raised in New York City where she completed her education and college and started her career. She made the move to California when she founded her first company in advertising. After a decade in that industry—and experiencing both the highs and lows of the field—she decided to go back to school for her Masters in Business Administration and attended a program in California that specialized in sustainability, also called a "Green MBA." She then shifted her focus from building companies to helping social entrepreneurs grow and scale. Shonda has helped more than a hundred companies expand from a handful of team members to mid-size operations by finding new market opportunities and ways to scale production and manufacturing while still staying aligned with the company mission. Shonda often speaks and writes about social entrepreneurship. She serves as a mentor in a few incubator programs focused on social enterprise and, schedule-permitting, teaches a course on global social entrepreneurship at a local university.

Shonda answers the call and Sara is thrilled that Shonda is in town for the next few weeks. They decide to meet up the next morning.

* * *

Over steaming cups of coffee and tea the next morning, Shonda and Sara do some initial catching up and then jump right into Sara's questions:

> *Sara:* "I've heard the phrase a few times, but wanted to ask you—"

2 WHAT IS SOCIAL INNOVATION?

Sara, let me say first—I am so happy to hear you are launching a business. It takes guts and courage. I want you to remember that on those days when everything seems to be going wrong or breaking!

Okay, then. Let's talk about social innovation; it is an important concept. And I recommend that you ask this question often and to a range of different people connected to the space—there isn't yet a singular definition of social innovation. It is an amalgam of ideas and concepts.

Broadly, social innovation leverages innovation (like innovation in technology, business, manufacturing, agriculture, communication, operations, etc.) to create positive social impact. Social innovation, in contrast with innovation on its own, is thought to create solutions that are more sustainable, efficient, just, or effective than existing solutions—and that benefit societies rather than only individuals or corporations.[11]

---

11 http://www.gsb.stanford.edu/faculty-research/centers-initiatives/csi/defining-social-innovation

Listen, Sara—think of social innovation like an umbrella. A big, old, yellow umbrella—one of those enormous kinds. Under the umbrella, you'll find more specific instances and subcategories of social innovation, like social enterprise, social entrepreneurship, cleantech, base-of-the-pyramid solutions, microfinance, and other specific articulations of social innovation. You might not know all of those "subcategories" yet, but that's what keeps this field exciting. As impact-driven entrepreneurs like you and your co-founders look at a pressing problem, you might come up with a whole new type of business model or way of solving it.

And the term social innovation is gaining popularity in a few big ways. In 2003, Stanford University introduced the *Stanford Social Innovation Review* as a print magazine focused on the emerging multi-disciplinary approach to addressing pressing societal needs and innovative solutions to address them; and within a year SSIR launched an accompanying website.[12] Together, the magazine, blog, and website have featured over 1,000 articles on social innovation and have made SSIR a popular resource for academics, practitioners, entrepreneurs, and students.[13] In 2010, the US established a new office—White House Office of Social Innovation and Civic Participation—and in 2010 created the Social Innovation Fund[14], which has awarded over $240 million in federal grants and more than $516 million in non-federal matching grants to organizations mobilizing private resources to find and grow community solutions with evidence-based results.[15]

A few other countries, including the United Kingdom, Malaysia, and South Africa, along with the European Union, are also beginning to recognize social innovation at a policy level.

12 http://ssir.org/
13 http://www.innov8social.com/2011/10/get-to-know-stanford-social-innovation
14 https://www.whitehouse.gov/administration/eop/sicp/initiatives/social-innovation-fund
15 http://www.nationalservice.gov/programs/social-innovation-fund

3 WHAT EXACTLY IS SOCIAL ENTREPRENEURSHIP?

Well, I'll tell you how I define it. Under the umbrella of social innovation sits social entrepreneurship. And believe me, it's a force to reckon with.

Social entrepreneurship harnesses the power and potential of business and enterprise to create both impact and profit. The term *social entrepreneurship* is often also used to describe the problem-solving mindset of addressing local and global problems with a business approach of identifying specific markets and leveraging business and financial models to achieve success. In that broader definition, a nonprofit or government agency could take a social entrepreneurship approach to problem-solving.

And here's a bit of historical background on social entrepreneurship. In 1980, Bill Drayton, who had been a schoolteacher in New York before going to Harvard and law school at Yale, founded the organization Ashoka.[16] In doing so, he challenged the idea of how we create impact. As a result of his influence, we now think about business models differently. Mr. Drayton is often recognized for popularizing the term "social entrepreneur" in the U.S. in the 1970s.[17] Ashoka is now the largest network of social entrepreneurs globally. Ashoka Fellows have gone on to create incredible ripples of impact around the world—and be recognized for it too. A number of past fellows have been awarded prestigious awards including the MacArthur "Genius" Grant, Buckminster Fuller Challenge, International Women of Courage Award, UNESCO awards, and even the Nobel Peace Prize.[18]

Let me tell you, these days, it seems like everybody wants to

---

16 Ashoka.org: About. Retrieved from https://www.ashoka.org/about
17 "Social Innovation, Evolving to Law". Parekh, Neetal. *Stanford Social Innovation Review*. Retrieved from http://ssir.org/articles/entry/social_innovation_evolving_to_law
18 Ashoa.org: Awards. Retrieved from https://www.ashoka.org/awards.

call themselves a social entrepreneur. Generally, though, it is used to refer to entities (for-profit or nonprofit) that are using business models to create impact.

Many people seem to use terms like *social innovation* and *social entrepreneurship* synonymously, and while there is a great deal of overlap, the terms have a slightly different connotation. Social innovation focuses more on *what* is being implemented, like a new technology or new process, to create impact. Social entrepreneurship focuses more on *how* it is being implemented, like with a business approach or leveraging a unique business model to create, grow, and scale both impact and revenue.

Also, oftentimes with social entrepreneurship there is a focus on being able to *scale*. That just means whether a company can go, for example, from selling 100 units of something to 1 million units of it. Or whether a social enterprise can pursue a model that goes from providing clean water to 10 families in an area to doing so for 100,000 families.

> *Sara:* "That's exactly the thing. I notice that some of the terms in the space seem like they have very similar definitions. For example…"

4 WHAT IS SOCIAL ENTERPRISE—HOW IS IT DIFFERENT FROM SOCIAL INNOVATION AND SOCIAL ENTREPRENEURSHIP?

Social enterprise often refers to for-profit companies that have an impact-related mission. In that way, a social enterprise would be the business, and the social entrepreneurs would be the founders or team members.

Social enterprise is often used as a generalized term that can include not-for-profit entities, too. Sometimes you might hear social enterprises say they are "impact/mission first." That is a way to signify that the basis or essence of their company is rooted in social impact. As the spectrum broadens and more companies use terms like social enterprise to describe themselves, the industry is finding ways to distinguish these "impact first" companies from companies with "impact too" or "impact as well" goals.

However, some countries use terms such as social enterprise much more specifically.

For example, countries including South Korea, Vietnam, Finland, and Italy have actually passed laws that define what a social enterprise is in those countries—so you can't just describe any business trying to create impact there as a "social enterprise."[19]

Social innovation as a sector is growing, emerging, and constantly evolving—and you can see that with what you have picked up on as the overlap of terms. There is increasing interest in the intersection of impact and value, and over time these terms will likely take on more distinct and consistent definitions as well.

Does that make sense?

> *Sara:* "It does. Social innovation is the big, yellow umbrella. Under it are other terms like social enterprise and social entrepreneurship. Social enterprises in some countries have specific definitions, but in places like the U.S. the term is used more broadly to mean companies that have dual goals of creating impact and profit. Thanks, that was super helpful. I've been finding these terms a lot in my research—and now I can see how they are related but not exactly the same thing!"

> *Shonda:* "Exactly. Okay, I'm ready for your next question."

19 https://en.wikipedia.org/wiki/Social_enterprise

5 WHAT IS A SOCIAL BUSINESS—IS IT THE SAME AS A SOCIAL ENTERPRISE?

Here there *is* a more specific definition! For it to make sense, you have to know a bit about Muhammad Yunus.[20] Professor Yunus and the Grameen Bank won the Nobel Peace Prize in 2006. Yunus founded the Grameen Bank, a microfinance institution, in Bangladesh. Professor Yunus and the bank won for showing how small loans and credit lines can create impact. He is an active entrepreneur and is often called the father of microfinance.[21] Professor Yunus has written a number of books on social impact, and he has made efforts to specifically define a "social business" and distinguish it from the other terms commonly used to describe businesses that seek to create both social impact and profit.

Essentially, for Professor Yunus, a social business is one that is completely committed to achieving a social objective, so while not operating at a loss, it also doesn't hand out dividends beyond initial investments made to the company.[22]

Professor Yunus specifically defines two types of social businesses: Type I and Type II.[23]

Type I Social Business

According to Professor Yunus, a Type I social business is focused on social objectives. It either produces a product or delivers a service targeted to the poor or to addressing a pressing problem. An example he discusses at length in the book *Building Social Business* is that of Shakti Doi, a yogurt fortified with vitamins and minerals designed to improve

20 CV of Professor Muhammad Yunus [Yunus Centre]
21 http://www.smh.com.au/national/access-to-credit--a-human-right-says-the-father-of-microfinance-20141010-113j3x.html
22 Yunus, M. (2007, December 25). Social Business. Retrieved from http://www.muhammadyunus.org/index.php/social-business/social-business
23 *What is Social Business? Defined by Nobel Peace Prize Laureate and Father of Microfinance, Muhammad Yunus* [Video]. Innov8social. (2015). Retrieved from http://www.innov8social.com/2015/06/what-is-social-business-defined-by

nutrition for malnourished children in Bangladesh. The yogurt is the result of a joint venture between Yunus' Grameen Bank and the multinational brand Danone.

Multiple iterations of the yogurt were tested to maximize nutrients while ensuring the cost was low enough (for example, it was originally sold at 5 Bangladeshi Taka, around $0.07 US, to ensure that the ventures met Yunus' vision of a true social business).[24]

Type II Social Business

Type II social businesses can adopt a profit-maximizing, dividend-generating model, as long as they are owned by the poor and disadvantaged. The profits can be returned to the owners or employees through dividends or indirect benefits.

The most famous example of a Type II social business is the Grameen Bank itself because it is owned by the disadvantaged borrowers of the bank, who are mostly women.

In Professor Yunus' book, *Building Social Business*, he clearly articulates that there can be a contradiction in constantly seeking to grow a business and gain revenue when your main purpose is to provide the most affordable, best-quality products and services to the poorest people.

> *Sara:* "Okay, so I actually had no idea that a social business had such a specific definition. I'm glad I found that out so I don't use it to mean a social enterprise. I need to look into social businesses in the U.S. and globally, but I still have some questions about social enterprises."

> *Shonda:* "Well, that's what I'm here for. Have at it!"

---

24 Yunus, M. (2010). *Building Social Business: The New Kind of Capitalism That Serves Humanity's Most Pressing Needs.* Public Affairs.

6 WHAT ARE EXAMPLES OF SOCIAL ENTERPRISES IN THE U.S.?

There are some pretty fascinating examples of social enterprise, and the sector is expanding. I can tell you about a few different kinds of social enterprises so you get an idea of the breadth and scope of businesses in this space.

Back to the Roots

Back to the Roots is one of my favorite stories.[25] It initially became famous for repurposing waste products to create sustainable food, and it has a pretty great startup story too. It was started by Nikhil Arora and Alejandro Velez when they were college seniors at UC Berkeley in 2009. They heard from a professor that you could create gourmet mushrooms from coffee grounds and had to try it out. After getting some pretty impressive results, they decided to launch an organic mushroom company that repurposed spent coffee grounds (i.e., waste) and incubated spores to eventually produce locally, sustainably-grown gourmet mushrooms.

Nikhil and Alejandro perfected the process so they could incubate the spore and then sell a kit where the end user would just have to spritz the spore with water for a few days for the mushrooms to begin growing. The high quality and affordability of the at-home mushroom kit made it a hit with major retailers like Whole Foods and Home Depot.

The founders, Nikhil and Alejandro, are passionate social enterprise advocates. They supported legislation for new legal structures for social ventures. And they met President Obama to discuss entrepreneurship and expanding the vision of their company to educate and grow sustainable food. Their second

---

25 http://www.innov8social.com/2013/02/interview-with-nikhil-arora-and

product is an aquaponics fish tank and herb-growing kit where herbs grow on top of a tank fertilized by live fish. This living ecosystem is not only a fun way to learn about the food cycle, but it also creates a sustainable source of locally-grown food.

Back to the Roots is a fascinating story about a mission-driven business that has found a way to repurpose waste products to create value and the constant innovation and social entrepreneur mindset needed to keep growing and broadening a business.

The Back to the Roots team is also active in educating kids and students about farming and growing local, sustainable food. In 2015, Back to the Roots received $2 million in seed investment[26] from a group of angel investors—i.e., funders who fund early-stage companies when the return on investment is not really clear—with expertise in the food industry, including folks from companies like Annie's Inc., Clif Bar, Stonyfield Farm, Jamba Juice, and TOMS.

There are other companies that come to mind when you say "social enterprise." The caveat, of course, is that people define social enterprises differently.

TOMS

TOMS, originally TOMS Shoes, is poised to become one of the largest, most profitable value-based ventures in the U.S. Some have said it may be the first $1 billion social enterprise.[27]

It was founded in 2006 by Blake Mycoskie, a Texas-based entrepreneur and participant in the 2002 season of the reality show *The Amazing Race*. The show took him and his sister (his teammate) through Argentina. He returned a few years

26 Kolodny, L. (2015, June 9). Back to the Roots Raises $2 Million to Grow Its Mini-Gardens, Food Brand. *Wall Street Journal*. Retrieved from http://blogs.wsj.com/venturecapital/2015/06/09/back-to-the-roots-raises-2-million-to-grow-its-mini-gardens-food-brand/
27 Kaplan, A. (2014, August 22). America's First Billion-Dollar Social Enterprise? *Huffington Post*. Retrieved from http://www.huffingtonpost.com/auren-kaplan/the-worlds-first-billion-_b_5697922.html

later and noted a few things. One was that many people in Argentina were wearing a certain type of comfortable shoe that had been worn by Argentinian farmers for centuries. The second was that many kids in rural or impoverished areas of Argentina did not wear shoes at all.

These observations became the design and impact inspiration behind the company he started. Core to its value proposition is "one-for-one," where for one item purchased, another item is given to a child in need. TOMS may have started out with shoes, but the company has now branched out to other consumer goods including eyewear and coffee roasting.

TOMS received some notable press and media coverage by way of the *Los Angeles Times*[28] and *Vogue*[29] early on that helped the company gain traction in big ways. It has been the choice footwear for notable celebrities and has made its founder into a kind of ambassador for business models for social impact. As of 2015, TOMS has given over 45 million pairs of shoes to children in need.

But here I have to add that TOMS is also a good example of how different people define social enterprise and some of the open questions in the space. Some people question the true social impact of giving away a consumer good like shoes,[30] versus addressing the root cause of the lack of shoes. Does that make sense?

I think it's an important discussion to have. I also think that we can't deny the incredible impact that companies like TOMS can make by their mere existence, and for TOMS, by their great success. It can be improved, sure, but as an entrepreneur, I'm of the camp that you gotta start somewhere!

---

28 Moore, B. (2009, April 19). Toms Shoes' model is sell a pair, give a pair away. *Los Angeles Times*. Retrieved from http://www.latimes.com/fashion/alltherage/la-ig-greentoms19-2009apr19-story.html
29 http://www.inc.com/jill-krasny/hilarious-story-of-how-toms-shoes-got-into-nordstroms.html
30 Herrera, A. (2013, March 19). Questioning TOMS Shoes Model for Social Enterprise. *New York Times*. Retrieved from http://boss.blogs.nytimes.com/2013/03/19/questioning-the-toms-shoes-model-for-social-enterprise/?_r=0

Etsy

Etsy is a fascinating and evolving story of a mission-aligned venture that scaled from its startup phase to a public company with the intent of retaining its mission. Etsy was founded in 2005 as an online marketplace for creative entrepreneurs to make, buy, and sell unique goods. Originally it had a rule that everything posted for sale had to be handmade by the seller, but shed the rule in 2013. In April 2015, Etsy had an initial public offering (IPO) where it made the company public and sold over $260 million of shares.[31]

Etsy is a certified B corporation, signifying its commitment to creating positive social impact for the community and environment in addition to shareholders. The company has reiterated its commitment to creating impact and maintaining its status as a B corporation.

As a certified B corporation that has had an IPO, Etsy is obligated to re-incorporate as one of the new legal forms—benefit corporation—likely by 2017, to retain its status with the B/benefit corporation movement.[32]

As companies like Etsy scale and grow, we see questioning of practices that may be common for traditional corporations but are called into question for impact-aligned companies. For example, in 2015 Etsy's tax strategy of lowering taxation by moving some of its intellectual property to Ireland has been met with differing opinions. Some point to large corporations such as Google, Microsoft, and Apple which do the same and note that Etsy still retains a strong impact rating according to the B Lab Impact Assessment. Others find Etsy's actions counter to its mission to create positive social impact and even call for its B corporation certification to be reviewed and potentially repealed.[33]

---

31 21 Fast Facts about the Etsy IPO, a Certified B Corporation. (2015, May 5). Retrieved from http://www.innov8social.com/2015/05/21-fast-facts-about-etsy-ipo-certified
32 Blog I Meant to Write #2: Etsy IPO. (2015, April 23) http://www.theconglomerate.org/2015/04/blog-i-meant-to-write-2.html
33 Could Etsy Lose This Beneficial Competitive Advantage? (2015, Sept 9). Retrieved from http://www.fool.com/investing/general/2015/09/12/could-etsy-lose-this-beneficial-competitive-advant.aspx

The debate is valuable, and with very few certified B corps having had an IPO, there is no clear answer. Moreover, Etsy's response or actions may set a precedent for how other scaling impact companies conduct businesses and taxes ahead too.

> *Sara:* Okay, those companies are very interesting and map out different sectors in the space! But I'm wondering how nonprofits fit into the picture.

7 CAN A NONPROFIT ORGANIZATION BE A SOCIAL ENTERPRISE?

Remember when I said to ask about the definition of social entrepreneurship early and often? Well, here's a perfect example of why. Depending on who you speak to and the context, some nonprofit organizations also align themselves with the term social enterprise. And in some cases, it is for a good reason.

For example, take D-Rev. It is a product development company structured as a nonprofit.

D-Rev

Short for "Design Revolution", D-Rev is a design company that serves customers that live on less than $4 per day. Structured as a nonprofit, D-Rev focuses on designing products that either improve health or increase income.[34]

D-Rev is particularly interested in serving, i.e., selling to, the base of the pyramid. This is a term you should know: the *base or bottom of the pyramid (aka BOP)* is the socio-economic group representing the poorest of the poor globally. This, broadly speaking, is the 3.5 billion people worldwide who live on less than $3 per day.[35]

34 Designing for social impact: The D-Rev story. (2014, June). Retrieved from http://www.mckinsey.com/insights/social_sector/designing_for_social_impact_the_d_rev_story
35 Shah, A. (2013, January 7). Poverty Facts and Stats. Retrieved from http://www.globalissues.org/article/26/poverty-facts-and-stats

Two products that D-Rev has designed to serve the BOP include:

- Brilliance phototherapy technology to treat jaundiced babies. While a phototherapy device typically costs $3500, D-Rev has designed one that performs just as well, or even better, for $400.[36]

- ReMotion knee, a prosthetic knee designed for above-knee amputees. The restoration of use of a limb such as a leg enables individuals to earn a livelihood, use a bicycle to travel, and otherwise regain mobility in ways that can materially change quality of life. While prosthetic knees can cost $6,000, D-Rev has designed one for $80.[37]

As the organization scales its designs, it is also seeing the need to engage in more than just design by involving itself in the distribution, sales, training, and management of product life cycles. They have seen from their past work that designing a great product is not enough to create systemic change. They need to be involved every step of the way to ensure that the low-cost product remains low-cost by the time it reaches the end user and beneficiary.

As a product development company, D-Rev does have sales and revenues; however, it has opted not to use these to profit the company but rather integrates any revenues back into the company and cause.

Just so that terms stay clear, I would call the founders social entrepreneurs engaging in an important social innovation. I would, however, qualify the use of the term social enterprise by specifying that is a "nonprofit social enterprise" to avoid confusion.

---

36 Newborn Health Impact Dashboard. Retrieved from http://d-rev.org/impact/brilliance/
37 Mobility Impact Dashboard. Retrieved from http://d-rev.org/impact/remotion/

Sara: "So, Shonda, as I mentioned earlier, my co-founders and I are exploring starting a company that has both a mission and business impact. We met at a workshop with lots of other aspiring social entrepreneurs and I guess I'm wondering—"

8 WHAT DO YOU HAVE TO DO TO BECOME A SOCIAL ENTERPRISE?

Depending on which country you are in, you likely don't have to *do* anything to use the term social enterprise. In many places, the term is used very broadly. But if you do self-identify as a social enterprise, be ready to be challenged on your mission, how you measure and assess impact, and how you remain a viable enterprise.

In certain places, like South Korea, a social enterprise is defined by the government.[38] An organization (nonprofit or for-profit) must register with the government in order to use the term social enterprise. So depending on where you are incorporating, it's a good idea to check local and federal laws to learn about any specific implications for using the term.

The benefits of embracing the term *social enterprise* include finding like-minded people and entrepreneurs who can help you achieve your goals and be a support system as you navigate through common questions such as legal formation, fundraising, impact measurement, and so on. It takes a village to impact a village—so everyone has a role to play. Additionally, identifying as a social enterprise may connect you with your target market: conscious and informed consumers who are looking to "vote" for companies they believe in with their purchases and patronage.

---

38 For more on social enterprise in South Korea, see Social Enterprise in South Korea: 5 Facts. (2015, January 11). Retrieved from http://www.innov8social.com/2015/01/social-enterprise-in-south-korea-5-facts

Sara: "Ok, that makes sense. I sometimes see stamps or seals on products I buy, and I was wondering..."

9 WHAT DO STAMPS, SEALS, AND CERTIFICATIONS LIKE "B CORP", "CRADLE-TO-CRADLE", AND "FAIR TRADE" SIGNIFY? SHOULD MISSION-DRIVEN COMPANIES PURSUE THESE SEALS?

There are a host of certifications that are available, with new ones emerging, to denote meeting certain criteria or conditions. They might explain how the company sources raw materials (e.g., fair-trade certified),[39] or whether a building was built with best practices for environmental sustainability (e.g., Leadership in Energy and Environmental Design, aka LEED certification).[40]

Other certifications denote some process or design-oriented thinking that may reduce waste (e.g., Cradle-to-Cradle Certified)[41] or may convey something about the ingredients (e.g., "certified organic").

These certifications tend to align with the concept of the "triple bottom line." It is a kind of expansion and also response to the traditional "bottom line" of a company, which refers to its net income, net revenue, or earnings per share.

Triple bottom line

A triple bottom line:

- focuses on the stakeholders impacted by a company, including people, planet, and profits.

- is used by companies that want to 1) maximize impact to their consumers or the local community, 2) reduce waste

39 See http://fairtradeusa.org/certification
40 See http://www.usgbc.org/leed
41 Visit http://www.c2ccertified.org/get-certified/product-certification

and consider the environment; and 3) generate profit and be sustainable.

I can outline a few social impact certifications, "quality labels," or "ecolabels" as they can be called. For a great, comprehensive list, you can also check out ecolabelindex.com/ecolabels to see a listing of more than 459 ecolabel listings and get sense of the attributes and requirements of each.

Certified

B

Corporation

B Corporation Certification (B Corp)

The B Corporation certification (also known as "B corp") was established in 2006 to recognize companies that meet specific minimum standards of social and environmental performance, accountability, and transparency.[42]

B corps (as certified B corporations are called) are a growing *global* community of companies. There are over 1400 B corps from over 40 countries. They have local meetups and even broad scale retreats for member companies. Additionally, member B corps are listed in the B corp directory online. As you can see, the B corp certification is more public facing—so for companies that really want to show their consumers that they are sustainability and impact focused, the B corp certification lets them wear it like a badge, literally!

Certifying as a B corporation requires:

- a self-assessment that scores within the required range

- a fee of $500 to $50,000 annually, based on the total annual sales of the company, to maintain the certification and display

---

42 For more on B corporations, see https://www.bcorporation.net

the "B corp" seal on the company's website and packaging.

• recertification every two years

• random audits by B Lab, the certifying nonprofit organization. B Lab can repeal a certification if a company is not measuring up to the minimum standards.

There is a comprehensive book out about B Corps by sustainability consultant Ryan Honeyman, who has worked with dozens of B corps. It is called *The B Corp Handbook* and has detailed information about the B corporation certification process and profiles of a variety of B corps.[43]

Cradle to Cradle Certification[44]

The Cradle to Cradle Certified(CM) Products Program provides a company with a means to demonstrate efforts in eco-intelligent design. The concept of "cradle to cradle" design is further detailed in the books *Cradle to Cradle: Remaking the Way We Make Things* and *The Upcycle: Designing for Abundance*,[45] which focus on ecologically intelligent design, i.e., design that acknowledges the lifecycles of products and anticipates how a product can reduce or eliminate waste at the end of its lifecycle.

Cradle to Cradle certification adopts a five-tiered approach: Basic, Bronze, Silver, Gold, and Platinum levels. It applies to materials, sub-assemblies, and finished products.

43 https://www.bcorporation.net/handbook
44 http://www.c2ccertified.org/images/uploads/V3_Transition_010813.pdf
45 To read more about the books, see http://www.mbdc.com/cradle-to-cradle/cradle-to-cradle-book/

The primary criteria considered for the certification include:

- use of materials that are safe for human health and the environment through all use phases

- product and system design for material reutilization, such as recycling or composting

- use of renewable energy

- use of water that is efficient, and maximum water quality associated with production

- consideration of company strategies for social responsibility

Fairtrade

Fairtrade certification means that the producers and traders have met prescribed Fairtrade standards, including social, environmental, and economic criteria, as well progress requirements and terms of trade. The standards are designed to support the sustainable development of small-scale producers and agricultural workers in the poorest countries in the world. Established in 1997, it is administered by 25 international organizations in over 112 countries.

There are distinct standards for individual industries including for[46]:

- small producer organizations

- hired labor

---

46 http://www.fairtrade.net/our-standards.html

- contract production

- traders

Here is a sampling of other certifications listed on ecolabelindex.com:

The Carbon Footprint of Products (CFP) is a system, primarily used in Japan, which displays the carbon footprint of products on the packaging, allowing consumers to obtain reliable information about GHG emissions and make informed decisions.

Certified Humane Raised and Handled is designed to certify that animals raised for dairy, lamb, poultry, and beef products are treated in a humane manner. For this certification, growth hormones are prohibited and animals are raised on a diet without antibiotics. They also have access to clean and sufficient food and water. A safe and healthful living environment is also required from birth through slaughter.

ENERGY STAR is the national symbol (currently in US and South Africa) for energy efficiency. Products that earn the ENERGY STAR mark prevent greenhouse gas emissions by meeting strict energy-efficiency guidelines set by the U.S. Environmental Protection Agency.

Since its inception in 1989, Green Seal has certified thousands of products and services that meet science-based environmental standards. It utilizes a lifecycle approach to ensure tangible reductions in the whole environmental footprint. Products must meet minimum standards and are subject to an on-site audit. They are ANSI-accredited and meet ISO and GEN requirements.

The LEED Green Building Rating System™ (i.e. The Leadership in Energy and Environmental Design) focuses on global adoption of sustainable green building and development practices. To receive LEED certification, building projects must satisfy prerequisites and earn points to achieve different levels (4 levels total) of certification.

The Marine Stewardship Council (MSC) fisheries standard can be found in over 60 countries. Fisheries must satisfy 3 core principles to qualify: 1) fish stocks must be sustainable; 2) fishing operations must minimize environmental impact; and 3) fisheries must meet all related local, national, and international laws.

TerraCycle runs national waste collection programs in 10 countries where non-recyclable post-consumer waste (i.e. used candy wrappers, toothbrushes, pens, juice pouches and many other categories of waste) is collected and made into new products and materials. The TerraCycle logo informs a consumer that the product or package is no longer waste and can be collected and sent (postage paid) to TerraCycle. Globally, TerraCycle has over 60,000 proprietary collection locations and over 12 million people participating in its waste collection programs.

If you think a particular certification may convey your mission effectively to your consumers, employees, funders, or partners, obtaining that certification may be worth considering. As you can see, certifications can align all aspects of your business with your stated mission and serve as a constant reminder of your commitment. On the flip side, if you are an early-stage social enterprise startup that is just trying to make it as a company, you may choose to wait on "investing" in pursuing a certification. Overall, the decision is really based on your core value proposition, and whether you and your co-founders believe this will be valuable at this particular stage of your business.

> *Sara:* "Thank you again, Shonda. This is all super helpful. I didn't realize there were so many moving parts to social entrepreneurship".

> *Shonda:* "You bet. The sector is growing and evolving a lot. I feel like there's some new definition or key concept popping up whenever I go to conferences or read new articles. I want to make sure I answered your questions. What else is on your mind?"

> *Sara:* "Well, yes. I have been reading a lot of blogs on this topic and have taken a few online classes on social entrepreneurship. One thing I would like to know about is the connection of CSR and social enterprise."

10 WHAT IS THE DIFFERENCE BETWEEN CORPORATE SOCIAL RESPONSIBILITY (CSR) AND SOCIAL ENTERPRISE?

That's a really important question, especially because just as we have a growing contingent of social entrepreneurs, a growing number of corporations are also becoming more attentive to measuring and reporting their social impact. In fact, looking down the road, we may see the lines blur between CSR and the kinds of social enterprise we have been talking about.

Right now though, one way to distinguish the two is to think about the role impact plays. Is the company "impact first," i.e., impact is the primary goal or on par with profit, or is impact considered after the company pursues a strong bottom line? If the organization is "impact first," then it suggests a social enterprise. If impact is secondary, then you're likely looking at corporate social responsibility measures that leverage a corporation's resources, workforce, products, and services for charitable or social impact initiatives.

CSR

Maybe you're wondering what CSR actually looks like. More and more corporations each year are releasing Sustainability or Impact Reports. Seeing some of these can contextualize the disruptive role that CSR plays in the social impact sector.

Take Walmart, for example. It is currently the world's largest retailer and the go-to place for 25% of Americans (and closer to 50% of 29 markets worldwide) to buy their groceries. It has 11,000 retail locations, employs more than 2 million people, and contracts with thousands of suppliers who, in turn, employ millions.[47] You can see that even small shifts in the Walmart Supply Chain can ripple to create massive impact. And that's how CSR initiatives can mean big-time net impact.

According to Walmart's 2015 Global Responsibility Report, the company estimated sourcing goods from 1 million farmers from emerging markets globally and giving $1 billion in food contributions to address hunger alleviation by the close of the year.[48] Few, if any, companies could ever scale the kind of impact that a huge, global company like Walmart can with a few tweaks to their manufacturing, production, sourcing, or distribution.

CSR is a fascinating field and plays a critical role in the

47 Holt, S. (2015, June 5). Walmart's Sustainability Promises: Myth vs. Reality. Retrieved from http://civileats.com/2015/06/05/walmarts-sustainability-promises-myth-vs-reality/
48 Walmart's Global Responsibility Report. (2015). Retrieved from http://www.corporatereport.com/walmart/2015/grr/

ecosystem for social impact. The Global Reporting Initiative (GRI) maintains a database related to CSR called the "Sustainability Disclosure Database," featuring over 27,000 sustainability reports of nearly 9,000 corporations and organizations.[49] CSRWire has also been reporting on CSR news and reports since 1999.

CSR is vital and allows established companies to more easily engage in impact. However, social enterprises have an impact mission core to their value proposition and their identity. Therefore, whereas a social enterprise would not *exist* without its impact objective, a corporation in most of the world can *elect* how much or how little to engage in CSR initiatives.

The reason I say "in most of the world" is because in 2014, India became the first country to pass legislation requiring companies set aside 2% of net profits over the previous 3 years to CSR initiatives. It applies to about 8,000 companies in India: those with net worth of at least $80 million or net profit of at least $830,000. This amounts to about $2 billion set aside for CSR initiatives. That could prove to be a major game changer and could shift the role of CSR within social innovation.

> *Sara:* "Very interesting. I want to look into how social enterprise startups can work with companies as part of their CSR initiatives. That could be a real win-win! I do have a few questions for you about the business side of social enterprises."

11 HOW DO SOCIAL ENTERPRISES MAKE MONEY?

The short answer is, like every entrepreneur, they hustle!

Social enterprises generate revenue through sales, repeat

---

customers, partnerships, and effective business models. And just like other companies, some may find creative ways to generate revenue, including advertising, subscription, and membership services, and through the sale of data or reporting.

If you want see a helpful visual mapping of various ways big companies earn revenues, take a look at SEER Interactive's mapping of companies such as Google, Apple, Netflix, and Facebook, at http://rcs.seerinteractive.com/money/. It might help your team as you brainstorm options.

Earning revenue is critical for social enterprises. Beyond validating a business model, it can actually go toward validating the social enterprise's value proposition. Since the field is still growing, and much of the revenue generation for social enterprises can be modest, showing a solid sales record and growth can make a big difference to investors and funders.

So, as the saying goes "always be pitching" — and I add, "always be selling"!

12 WHAT ARE COMMON BUSINESS MODELS FOR SOCIAL ENTERPRISE?

In order to bake social impact into a new startup or business, social entrepreneurs have become more creative in thinking about business models. Here are a few business models that mission-driven companies are using.

- **Buy one, give one.** We talked about TOMS as an example of an impact company. This has been their business model and in all of their marketing from the start. The nice thing about a business model like this is that it's as easy to explain to your investors as it is to your customers and to your team! The simplicity can be a big plus when telling your story and mapping out impact goals.

- **Sliding scale / pay what you can.** This model has been employed by a number of social enterprises. One notable one is the Aravind Eye Care System in India.[50] It is a nonprofit social enterprise that performs sight-saving eye surgeries. Founded in 1976, Aravind has treated well over 32 million patients and performed more than 4 million surgeries.[51] In fact, according to it's 2014-2015 annual report,[52] Aravind medical teams at the 67 affiliated locations see over 15,000 patients and perform 1,500 surgeries on a *daily* basis.[53] It utilizes a low-cost, high-volume business model for eye surgery services. About 70% of eye surgeries are performed for free or below cost, while 30% are performed for above cost without compromising quality of care on either side of the price range.

- **Percentage models.** Salesforce popularized the 1-1-1 model. As a company that was not founded on impact, it is notable that this giving model has been implemented from its start. It means that the company gives away 1% of its product, employee time, and revenue to charitable causes and to the community. A social enterprise could use a percentage model such as Salesforce's to effectuate a commitment to impact. Another firm, verynice design, based in Los Angeles, uses a "Give Half" model in which 50% of design projects are completed pro bono for nonprofit or community clients.

There is an incredible and engaging online platform for researching business models for social enterprises called Models for Impact at modelsforimpact.co. It's a really valuable mapping of both product-based and service-based social ventures. Here are a few unique groupings of business models identified:

50 http://www.aravind.org/
51 https://en.wikipedia.org/wiki/Aravind_Eye_Hospitals
52 http://www.aravind.org/default/publicationscontent/publication
53 Aravind Eye Care System, Activity Report 2014-2015. Retrieved from http://pubhtml5.com/idml/ytds

- *Businesses that create social impact by the markets they serve.* For example, certain social enterprises create products and services specifically for low-income markets (i.e., D-Rev), developing markets (Awaaz.de), or for health service providers (Medic Mobile).

- *Businesses that create social impact by what they do with cash earned.* Some companies, for example, give 100% of their profits to charities (i.e., Charity: Water, Newman's Own) or give half of their profits and services to pro bono clients (impact rising, verynice design).

- *Businesses that create impact by sharing information.* These companies engage in open source software (i.e., Wikipedia, Moodle, Thingiverse) and provide free access, which can be incredibly impactful.

13 HOW SHOULD A SOCIAL ENTERPRISE CHOOSE A BUSINESS MODEL?

Now this may sound a bit counterintuitive, but my biggest piece of advice related to choosing a business model is to not get too attached.

A great concept to help you think about how to manage the moving parts of your startup is to consider the Lean Startup Method as described and explained in *The Lean Startup*.[54] The concepts there, such as building a minimum viable product (MVP), gathering valuable customer feedback, and being able to objectively and effectively reflect on the data to make small changes or integral pivots, could be a key mindset for your social enterprise's success.

If you focus on building a product your customers love and

---

54 http://theleanstartup.com/

that is impactful for beneficiaries, then you may simply have to try various business models to find a way to sell it and clients who can afford to pay for it.

If you have a great product, the business model is the easy part. But if your product is just mediocre, your business model won't help. You might be able to sell a subpar product once, but that buyer probably won't be back around a second time!

> *Sara:* "It's been incredible learning more about the basics of social innovation, social entrepreneurship, and social enterprise. I am even more excited to take the next steps to build our company."

CHAPTER 3

Law and Policy

SARA LEAVES THE CAFE and glances at her phone. It's nearly past lunchtime. She text messages her teammates:

Sara:

GREAT meeting with Shonda. She knows her stuff. Lots to catch up on. I want to map out a few business models that take into account ways we can measure impact and how we can grow. What's happening on your end?

Tino:

Good work. Let's all meet. When?

Jay:

Super! Will be useful to hear her answers. About to meet Mr. Marcelo—can we regroup right after?

Sara:

YES! Heading to IMPACTATHON HQ...meet you guys there. Good luck, Jay!

Tino:

Ok. Reminder, it's Day 2. Let's stay focused so we can work fast, fail faster, build something great.

Jay glances up from his phone. He'll have to ask Tino exactly what he meant by that later. For now, though, he is excited to meet Mr. Ian Marcelo, one of the attorneys who is a mentor at his law school's Startup Law clinic and who teaches an upper-division course on social enterprise law. With the clock counting down until their presentation, Jay was glad to see his email this morning and find out Mr. Marcelo could meet at his office in San Francisco before an afternoon client meeting.

Ian has been practicing law in San Francisco for the better part of twenty years. His dad moved from a small town in the Philippines and met his mom in Texas, where Ian was born. He did all of his schooling and college there and majored in philosophy before taking a sharp turn into law. He moved to California for law school and after passing the Bar exam stayed in the area. Ian specializes in startup law and legal structures. He helps early and mid-stage companies think about questions around their legal formation and options. He is passionate about the intersection of law, policy, and social impact and has been involved in a few policy initiatives related to social enterprise law.

> *Jay:* Hi, Mr. Marcelo. Thank you so much for meeting me! I have a ton of questions about legal formation for a social enterprise I am forming with two co-founders.

> *Ian:* Not a problem, Jay. We're not in class, so call me Ian! Glad to see your interest in learning more. I know you know this, but as a friendly reminder, this isn't legal advice. For that, going to your attorney is the best bet. Today, I want to share information and my own experience about the different legal structures and options available for your social impact venture.

> *Jay:* Great! As you know, we're exploring ways to create a company that creates profit and impact. The first question I wanted to find out is…

14 ARE THERE SPECIAL LEGAL STRUCTURES FOR SOCIAL ENTERPRISES?

There absolutely are. Companies based in the U.S. can choose between new legal structures or existing legal structures or combinations. They can also rely on established legal principles when deciding on how to move forward with forming their entities.

Off the bat, let's go through a few terms. A *hybrid structure* is the term cool kids are using these days to describe these new legal structures that combine elements of for-profit and nonprofit legal structures. An example of this is the benefit corporation—it's a single structure but formalizes aspects of nonprofit (i.e., commitment to impact) as well for-profit (i.e., generating revenue) organizations. Each of the structures does this a little differently, and in the U.S., each state recognizes its own version of these structures.

The term *tandem* is a good one to describe the use of multiple legal structures to achieve the intended goals, such as impact and profit. So a social enterprise could be structured as a C corporation and have a non-profit organization associated as well. Think of it like a tandem bicycle: multiple riders (or in our case, legal structures) working together for the same goals.

I have to warn you that folks sometimes use "tandem" to describe "hybrid," but for our conversation I'll use the terms as I just described them—namely, *hybrid*, to describe a single legal structure combining elements of nonprofit and for-profit entities, and *tandem* to describe the situation when multiple legal structures are used to achieve a social enterprise's goals.

Some of the existing legal structure options for mission-driven companies include cooperatives, limited liability companies (LLCs), C corporations, and nonprofit organizations.

A few of the new legal structures include benefit corporations, social purpose corporations, and low-profit limited
liability companies. Each structure, of course, has different ad-
vantages and drawbacks.

> *Jay:* Wow, those are more options than I realized. Let's start
> with cooperatives.

15 WHAT IS A COOPERATIVE—HOW IS IT USEFUL FOR A SOCIAL ENTERPRISE?

In broad brush strokes, cooperatives ("co-ops") can be described as companies owned by their members. I know you
guys are trying to learn enough about co-ops to decide whether it's the right legal structure for you. So, I'm going to break
it down and give you the top 5 things you should know about
co-ops and how they fit into social enterprise.

Co-ops

1. Co-ops can be legal structures, a type of entity, and/or a
   shared set of values.

2. There are different types of co-ops. A few types include
   worker co-ops, buyer co-ops, and social co-ops (currently only in Italy).

3. Co-ops are inherently democratic and distribute wealth
   equitably.

4. Co-ops align participant owners with a common mission.

5. Co-ops can be harder to scale and can deter outside
   funds, including venture capital.

Depending on how the cooperative is structured, each

member gets a vote. Janelle Orsi, co-founder of the Sustainable Economies Law Center http://www.theselc.org/, located in California, is the author of a book focused on the intersection of legal structure and social enterprise with a focus on cooperatives. Her book is called *Practicing Law in the Sharing Economy: Helping People Build Cooperatives, Social Enterprise, and Local Sustainable Economies.* She and her team have championed the cooperative as an equitable, effective legal form for social enterprises and have created a wealth of resources on co-ops on theselc.org and co-oplaw.org.[55]

Cooperatives also have a long history globally. Countries such as France, Ireland, Italy, and the UK have rich histories of cooperatives. Sweden, Finland, and Australia also have defined legal structures for co-ops.[56]

Jay: Okay, you mentioned LLCs and C corps—

16 HOW DO LLCS AND C CORPORATIONS WORK—CAN THEY PROTECT A SOCIAL ENTERPRISE'S MISSION WHILE STILL ENABLING IT TO PURSUE PROFIT?

LLCs

An LLC combines liability protection of a corporation with the pass-through taxation of a partnership. It is, in many senses, the "original hybrid" legal structure in the U.S. The owners of an LLC are called "members."

The LLC structure has its roots in late 19th century Germany, but the U.S. LLC structure was actually added fairly recently. It

---

55 Orsi, J. (2013). *Practicing Law in the Sharing Economy: Helping People Build Cooperatives, Social Enterprise, and Local Sustainable Economies.* American Bar Association.
56 For more on co-ops, see http://www.co-oplaw.org

was formed in the 1970s to provide a cost-effective legal form that didn't have as many formalities as the C corporation but still protected a company from liability.[57] Today, the LLC still provides those benefits. It is often used by professional corporations or consulting entities that are not seeking outside funding, like venture capital. For many startups, the goal is to scale and grow and to invite different types of funding. As a result, this tends to be a less popular form for startup companies looking to scale and grow. However, it remains a strong option for consulting companies or companies looking to quickly and affordably establish liability protection. As the company grows, and if it wants to issue stock, it will have to think about other forms.

C Corps

The traditional C corporation is the most common option for new startup companies. Investors like this form because it's familiar. As a side note, Delaware has laws that are favorable to corporations, so many startups incorporate in Delaware. Basically, since there have been many corporate law cases adjudicated in Delaware, the case law there has defined a lot of the nuances of corporate law. This makes the legal requirements and expectations more clear and known for both entrepreneurs and investors in instances of formation and exit (like with acquisition and IPO).

The C corporation has legal formalities and is considered a separate entity from its founders and employees. This "citizenship" means that directors and executives have a fiduciary duty to the corporation and shareholders. "Fiduciary duty" is the fancy-pants way of saying "legal duty."

---

57 Keatinge et al.,"The Limited Liability Company: A Study of the Emerging Entity," 47 Business Lawyer 375, 383-384 (Feb. 1992) (citing Act of 4 March 1977, ch. 155, 1977 Wyo.Sess.Laws 512).

A few key concepts will help add depth to the interesting aspects of C corporations for companies seeking to create impact in addition to profit.

- **Business Judgment Rule** is a legal principle that gives deference to business decisions made by directors of a company. It is supposed to protect decision makers in a company from shareholder lawsuits by giving some automatic trust to the judgment of a company's Board of Directors. It is based on the notion that company executives have a stake in the success of the company and thus would use such judgment in making decisions.[58]

- **The case of *Dodge v. Ford*** (1919) is one of the landmark cases used to show that corporations have a fiduciary duty to maximize shareholder wealth. In that case, Henry Ford chose not to pay dividends but reinvested profit into the company. His shareholders disagreed and believed that Ford had made a decision that compromised the assumption of the Business Judgment Rule that he was acting in the best interest of shareholders. (i.e., in legalese, that he "pierced the corporate veil"). In the end, the Michigan Supreme Court sided with the shareholders, and Ford was forced to pay a special dividend to shareholders.

- **The Constituency Statute.** About 32 states have passed constituency statutes, which formally allow companies to make decisions for reasons other than maximizing shareholder value. Though these statutes were not passed with social enterprise missions in mind, they can provide a buffer for impact companies to pursue a triple bottom line.[59]

---

58 For more on business judgment rule, see http://www.innov8social.com/2011/08/what-is-business-judgement-rule-how

59 For more on constituency statutes, see http://www.innov8social.com/2011/08/what-is-constituency-statute

Let's Connect the Dots on Corporate Law, Leading to a "Third Space" for Social Enterprise Law

As you can see from the definitions, a long-held tenet under U.S. corporate law is the duty of corporations (i.e., the *fiduciary* duty) to *maximize* shareholder wealth. The famous case of *Dodge vs. Ford* underlined this ultimate goal and duty of a company to its shareholders.[60]

This can create an interesting paradox for social enterprises that aim to pursue impact in addition to profit. From years of U.S. case law, the "Business Judgment Rule" has emerged as an outlet from the strict view on maximizing shareholder wealth as opposed to deferring to the decision-making of a corporation's directors. The BJR, as it is affectionately referred to by legal practitioners, law professors, and students of law, gives deference to a corporation for its decision-making. "Hey, we basically trust that you're doing what you're doing for a reason," is figuratively what a court says when it defends a corporation's actions under the concept of BJR.

Another outlet for corporations acting for purposes other than profit-maximization is the Constituency Statute. Also known as "stakeholder statutes," some form of constituency statute has been passed in more than half of the America's 50 states. These statutes formally enable corporations to consider non-shareholder considerations when making decisions.

While defined legal concepts such as the Business Judgment Rule and Constituency Statutes provide some solid protection for a social venture, there are still risks.

Corporations and corporate directors risk potential shareholder derivative suits. These are lawsuits brought by shareholders of a corporation against a third party (which can include a corporate director) for not upholding fiduciary duties. For example,

---

60 For more on maximizing shareholder wealth, see http://www.innov8social.com/2011/06/who-said-corporations-have-to-maximize

a corporation that values pursuing impact equally with pursuing profit, and is incorporated in a traditional legal form, may run the risk of a shareholder action protesting a disproportionate attention to company mission, especially in a state without a Constituency Statute.

Additionally, companies that have successfully pursued mission and profit run the risk of diluting mission in the instance of an acquisition. Under U.S. law, a company is bound to accept the highest share price for a proposed acquisition—even if the acquirer may not subscribe to, support, or champion the mission.

In social enterprise circles, the case of *Ben and Jerry's* has been discussed at length—with savvy opinions on either side.[61] In 2000, Ben and Jerry's, a mission-driven ice cream company when operated by its founders, was acquired by Unilever, a large corporation. The story goes that Unilever didn't actually champion the mission-driven approach that the co-founders did, but was offering the highest share price. For that reason, and in order to avoid liability from shareholders, Ben and Jerry's sold to an acquiring company that didn't promise to continue operating according to its social intent. Some argue that had a legal structure (such as benefit corporation, which will be explained ahead) been in place, Ben and Jerry's would have had the option to go with an acquirer more aligned with its mission. Others argue that existing corporate law would still have enabled Ben and Jerry's to have a choice.

Either way, the case and situation highlight a grey area for successful social enterprises who want to ensure their mission is continued—even, and especially, in the case of an exit.

An innovative answer to these social entrepreneurs' legal concerns has come in the form of these new legal structures that take a further step to formalize pursuing a double or triple bottom line.

---

61 Read http://ssir.org/articles/entry/the_truth_about_ben_and_jerrys, particularly the comments, and http://www.innov8social.com/2012/09/interesting-ssir-article-takes-anothe

17   WHAT IS A LOW-PROFIT LIMITED LIABILITY COMPANY (L3C)?

This is a really interesting one. It's one of the only legal structures I've heard of that has been repealed by a state. At one point, eleven states and two jurisdictions had passed L3C legal structure, but North Carolina abolished the L3C as of January 1, 2014. So, today that number is ten states and two jurisdictions. You'll get a better idea of why once you know the story.

L3C

This is a type of limited liability company (LLC) that identifies a specific socially beneficial mission much like a nonprofit organization does, but unlike a nonprofit, an L3C allows profits to be distributed to owners. Like traditional LLCs, L3Cs limit the personal liability of owners and aren't taxed like corporations.

L3C legislation is enacted as an amendment to a state's current LLC legislation rather than as a separate bill. One main point that L3Cs were created to address was the IRS requirement that private foundations only invest in for-profit enterprises that are IRS-sanctioned, program-related investments (PRIs). The due diligence that a foundation does in order to pursue a PRI can be very time-consuming and expensive. The L3C creators wanted to make PRIs easier and to get funding to social impact companies faster and with fewer hurdles. A good idea, no doubt!

The hope was that L3Cs, by virtue of the outlined charitable purpose, would automatically meet the IRS criteria as a PRI.

The thing is, the IRS hasn't done anything to officially and federally recognize the L3Cs as satisfying criteria for program-related investments. So the L3Cs are kind of hanging out like a palm up in the air waiting to be high-fived!

Without this "nod" from the IRS, the L3Cs, while symbolic,

don't actually save the foundations from the due diligence. This was one of the reasons that North Carolina cited when they voted to repeal the L3C[62] structure, though existing L3Cs can still use the designation.

18 WHAT IS A SOCIAL PURPOSE CORPORATION (SPC)?

As of the end of 2015, four states (Washington, California, Florida, and Minnesota) have passed legislation formalizing the Social Purpose Corporation (SPC) in those states.

SPC

The SPC is a hybrid legal structure that lets for-profit social enterprises pursue a specific social impact benefit and list it in their articles of incorporation.

The SPC addresses a few of the concerns I mentioned related to C corporations and the paradox of pursuing an impact motive when there might be legal obligation to maximize shareholder wealth.

The standard of pursuing a "specific benefit" in some senses lowers the bar a bit for companies, because they only need to report and account for the specific benefit they identified when incorporating. Supporters of this law say that it actually makes SPCs more actionable since companies can focus on a particular benefit rather than trying to create an overall, general benefit. Those critical of this legal structure suggest that the broadness in defining the social impact in the SPC context can create the potential for "greenwashing" — i.e. when a company overstates, misstates, or misleads about its commitment to social impact

62 Field, A. (2014, January 11). North Carolina Officially Abolishes the L3C. *Forbes*. Retrieved from http://www.forbes.com/sites/annefield/2014/01/11/north-carolina-officially-abolishes-the-l3c/

or the sustainability of its operations.[63] Greenwashing is often disseminated for and through PR and marketing efforts.

A few side notes: California first passed this as the "flexible purpose corporation" but then renamed it to "social purpose corporation" in 2015. Minnesota combined benefit corporations (more on that ahead) and social purpose corporations within one piece of legislation.[64]

19 WHAT IS A BENEFIT CORPORATION—HAVE MANY STATES HAVE PASSED THIS STRUCTURE?

Ok! This is the one that has been gaining some major momentum in the past few years.

Benefit Corporation

A benefit corporation is a hybrid legal structure that establishes a for-profit entity with the goal of creating net positive impact in addition to profit goals. It has passed in 31 states and jurisdictions, and another five states are actively working on passing a version (as of 2015).[65]

Here are a few things to keep in mind about benefit corporations:

1. Benefit corporations exist, in part, to create general public benefit.

2. Benefit corporations are generally identical to C corporations except for (i) public purpose (ii) transparency and (iii) accountability.[66]

---

63 Ho, Tina H. (2015) "Social Purpose Corporations: The Next Targets for Greenwashing Practices and Crowdfunding Scams," Seattle Journal for Social Justice: Vol. 13: Iss. 3, Article 14. Available at: http://digitalcommons.law.seattleu.edu/sjsj/vol13/iss3/14
64 For further discussion, see http://socentlaw.com/2015/03/new-and-improved-u-s-hybrids-map-with-hyperlinks-minnesota-is-purple-5/ and http://www.innov8social.com/2015/01/cas-flexible-purpose-corporation.
65 http://benefitcorp.net/policymakers/state-by-state-status
66 Montgomery, J. (2015, November 3). Benefit corporation legal structure [Email interview].

3. Each state has had to pass its own version, so there is no "garden variety" benefit corporation. You have to look into each state's version to understand the requirements.

4. There is, however, *model legislation*, kind of the "everything burrito" of what the B Lab envisioned for the legislation. A majority of the states that have passed benefit corporation law have adopted a version of the model legislation[67] (including California, New York, Florida, Nevada, and Pennsylvania). Other states, such as Delaware and Colorado, have passed versions that actually look more like the Social Purpose Corporation. Go figure!

5. The model legislation specifies that benefit corporations are trying to create "a material positive impact" which basically means that all things considered, the companies can report an overall positive impact on society and the environment.

6. What about accountability? How do you know if benefit corporations are creating a general public benefit? Most states (and the model legislation) require assessment of impact by an independent third party standard.[68]

7. The B Lab has a standard, the B Impact Assessment (online, free). And there are also a host of independent groups[69] that provide standards too, including: GRI, GoodGuide, Green Seal, and ISO 26000.

8. What about transparency? Well, most states require annual reporting, and some even specify that impact reports need to be publicly available (like on the company website).[70]

9. Benefit corporations also protect directors from liability when making triple bottom line decisions.[71] Many also

---

67 http://www.smithmoorelaw.com/webfiles/BCorpWebMap.pdf (source: http://smithmoorelaw.com/BCorp)
68 http://www.triplepundit.com/2012/03/third-party-standards-benefit-corporations/
69 http://benefitcorp.net/businesses/how-do-i-pick-third-party-standard
70 http://benefitcorp.net/businesses/benefit-corporation-reporting-requirements
71 Montgomery, J. (2015, November 3). Benefit corporation legal structure [Email interview].

allow corporations to bypass conventional corporate case law which obligates a company to accept the highest bidder's price in the instance of an acquisition.[72] A benefit corporation can choose an acquiring company that is aligned with its core impact mission. I.e. companies like Ben and Jerry's could be as deliberate in assessing their acquiring company as they were in establishing and pursuing a double or triple bottom line.[73]

10. There can be a lot to keep track of when trying to visualize and understand the various state laws for benefit corporations. Charts and mappings by BenefitCorp.net,[74] Smith Moore Law,[75] Suffolk University Law School,[76] and Belmont University[77] provide a deep dive into the differences and distinctions between each state's law.

It's an exciting time for benefit corporations and legal structures for social enterprise, for sure! And don't be fooled; it's not easy to get new legal structures passed in a state. But now we're on to the next challenge: letting people like you know about these options and not feel so overwhelmed by the choices.

Jay: To be honest, it is all a bit overwhelming; there are a lot of choices. And it's only a small part of everything we have to think about now as co-founders. We are trying to figure out everything from product development, business plan, marketing, and more—so you can imagine that legal structure is just one more decision we have to make. I know this is important and in the long run can really serve to protect the *reason* we are even starting a business like ours.

There's another thing related to benefit corporations I want to understand better...

---

72 http://benefitcorp.net/faq
73 http://www.greenmoneyjournal.com/march-2014/ice-cream/
74 http://benefitcorp.net/sites/default/files/documents/State%20by%20State%20Analysis.pdf
75 http://www.smithmoorelaw.com/webfiles/BCorpWebMap.pdf
76 http://papers.ssrn.com/sol3/papers.cfm?abstract_id=1561783
77 http://i8s.us/BelmontU_ComparingStatueStatutes

20 IS A BENEFIT CORPORATION THE SAME AS A B CORPORATION—CAN A COMPANY BE BOTH?

Good question! And please memorize this because you will spend part of your time as a co-founder of a social enterprise clarifying this to your investors, consumers, and team!

The short answer is No and Yes!

No, they are *not* the same.

A benefit corporation is a legal structure. B corporation is a certification.[78]

A company has to incorporate legally as a benefit corporation and satisfy state requirements to qualify. If a company is reincorporating into or out of a benefit corporation structure, most states will require a supermajority vote (i.e., ⅔ or more of shareholders).

B Corporation Certification

A company has to apply for B corporation certification,[79] meet specified minimum requirements on an impact assessment, and then pay a fee based on revenues to become certified. Recertification happens every two years.

Whereas the benefit corporation structure is available in certain US states, where it has been passed, B corps (as certified b corporations are known) are a *global* community. This global movement is comprised of over 1400 companies from over 40 countries, with a number of countries seeking to establish a presence ahead. B corps are certified by the nonprofit entity B Lab, which also advocates on behalf of, builds a public presence for, and organizes events and retreats to further the work of the growing B corps community.

---

78 http://benefitcorp.net/businesses/benefit-corporation-vs-certified-b-corp
79 https://www.bcorporation.net/become-a-b-corp/how-to-become-a-b-corp

Interestingly, and this is important to know, there is a legal link between B corps and benefit corporations. All Certified B corps are required to meet a legal requirement as part of their certification. The legal requirement is that they have to somehow expand the fiduciary duty of their directors to consider stakeholder interests in decisionmaking. This can be done in different ways. For example, an LLC can amend its operating agreement; or, a corporation can amend its articles of incorporation to reflect the expanded duty. One way to do that, then, is to reincorporate as a benefit corporation. Interestingly, B corps in the US that have an IPO may be obligated to incorporate as a benefit corporation within a specified time frame.[80]

As you may notice, the B corp certification is more public facing, with member companies listed publicly on an online directory.

To be sure though, B Lab — the certifying nonprofit organization — randomly audits companies and can repeal a certification if a company is not measuring up to the minimum standards.

Yes, a company *can* be both.

There's nothing preventing a company from incorporating as a benefit corporation and pursuing the B corp certification. Considerations are added cost and whether both are really necessary for your purposes.

21 ARE THERE TAX BENEFITS TO INCORPORATING AS ONE OF THE NEW HYBRID STRUCTURES?

Interestingly, there are no tax benefits at the state or federal level.

Though there is nothing in the works now, it isn't to say

---

80 https://www.bcorporation.net/become-a-b-corp/how-to-become-a-b-corp/legal-roadmap/corporation-legal-road-map

incentives couldn't be added if companies adopting these guidelines prove that by creating valuable impact, they are desirable or provide a benefit to the society and economy. A tax break or benefit would be a huge incentive for companies to consider these legal structures, but on the balance, it could attract companies that are more interested in the tax break than in actually creating the impact.

22 WHY WOULD A COMPANY CHOOSE TO INCORPORATE AS A BENEFIT CORPORATION OR SOCIAL PURPOSE CORPORATION VERSUS A TRADITIONAL LEGAL STRUCTURE?

That's a great question, and one that, frankly, is debated regularly at social enterprise law office water coolers across the country. The reason is that traditional structures actually do protect a company's Board of Directors in its decision-making under the Business Judgment Rule and/or Constituency Statutes like I mentioned earlier.

However, there is a perception that traditional corporate forms are still obligated to pursue traditional goals of a company, including maximizing shareholder wealth.

With social enterprises, a company's Board of Directors is serving not only the shareholders, but also the impact objectives. The thinking for some founders (and attorneys) is that if you really want to protect your mission and ensure that the impact motive prevails if the company is bought out by another company or has an IPO, then the best way to do that is with one of the hybrid legal structures that specifically provide those protections.

23   WHAT ARE DRAWBACKS OF INCORPORATING AS A HYBRID LEGAL STRUCTURE?

Yes! That's exactly the kind of question you need to be asking as a co-founder. Don't get me wrong, I am as fascinated by these new legal structures as the next social enterprise lawyer, but they might not be the best fit for every company. As an attorney, my job is to help startups find a structure that will be the best fit for their goals, objectives, and growth strategies.

So the big thing with the new legal structures is that **they haven't been tested in court.** That means there is no case law. To be honest, we don't know how courts will react or uphold the impact objectives. You always need people to raise their hands and be the first, but some companies may not want to be in such an undefined area of law. Additionally, since each state has passed its own version of these legal structures, each state has different requirements. One side note that bears mention is that while there is no definitive case law on this subject yet, Chief Justice of the Delaware Supreme Court, Leo Strine, has written articles on the topic, including one titled "Making It Easier for Directors To 'Do The Right Thing'?" in which he supports the idea that benefit corporation statutes have the potential to shift accountability and put actual power behind the idea that corporations should act responsibly.[81]

Another consideration is that some attorneys feel **it isn't necessary to opt for a new legal structure** because there is enough protection within the system (i.e., Business Judgment Rule, constituency statutes) and with the shift in consciousness of corporations towards CSR, there is a natural evolution of the corporation.[82] However, this "wait and see" mentality may not

---

81 Strine Jr., Leo E. (2014) "Making it Easier for Directors to 'Do the Right Thing'?," Harvard Business Law Review, Vol. 4, P. 235, 2014. Available at: http://corpgov.law.harvard.edu/2014/11/10/making-it-easier-for-directors-to-do-the-right-thing/
82 http://lawprofessors.typepad.com/business_law/2014/09/march-of-the-benefit-corporation-so-why-bother-isnt-the-business-judgment-rule-alive-and-well-part-i.html

be a good fit for every company as it leaves a few important considerations undefined.

Another thing to keep in mind is that the **transparency and accountability requirements** of the new social enterprise legal structures may not be in line with the company's policy for releasing information. Depending on the state of incorporation, incorporating as a benefit corporation may mean making information publicly available that a Board of Directors is not comfortable with.

An additional consideration is that a hybrid structure such as a benefit corporation or social purpose corporation **may not be ideal when seeking investment from traditional investors**. Investors, like venture capitalists, are used to C corporations and may not be familiar or comfortable with the dual motivations of a benefit corporation.

The **last thing to think about is cost**. There is a cost to incorporate, and if your company pursues both a certification and legal structure, you may be spending more than expected on structuring your sustainability initiatives, leaving a little less for other costs and expenses.

> *Jay:* "This is all really fascinating. Some other time, I would love to hear how you created your career in startup law and connected it to social impact. For now, though, there is a lot for us to think about. Thank you, and I can't wait to pass this info on to the team."

> *Ian:* "My pleasure, Jay! I want to hear what you guys decide. For now, though, I've gotta run! I have to get to the other end of the city for my next meeting. Good luck."

CHAPTER 4

Fundraising

TINO HAS BEEN BACK AT IMPACTATHON since late morning. He has had a chance to talk to various teams and learn about their ideas and approaches to social impact. He notices from participating and coaching in multiple hackathons that each team can be at a vastly different stage this early in the week.

Some teams, like D.Litter, which is building an app to gamify litter pick-up by offering rewards and prizes to people for cleaning up trash in their communities, are comprised almost entirely of engineers. And as Tino walks by, he sees two of the co-founders sporting enormous headphones and intently coding on their laptops. He sees another of the co-founders, Nirali, approaching her spot at the table.

Tino: "Hey Nirali, how is it going?"

Nirali: "Hi Tino! Good, I guess. It's so hard to tell with these hackathons, right? We started coding early this morning. Hopefully we can make some progress and have something by later this week. There are so many features we want to build. It's awesome and kind of overwhelming too."

Tino: "Ok, good that you're on the way to a prototype. But, why don't you just build the simplest version of the app so you can get it out to users *sooner*? You know, build it 'lean'. You're going to spend days working on it and you won't even know until the end of the week if it's something people want. What if it's not? You still need to have something to pitch on Saturday. Think about it."

Nirali: "Like the 'Lean Startup' method, right? Minimum viable product and all of that. It's a good idea. I think we've just started building up momentum for all of the coding, so we have to balance that motivation out with leaving enough time for customer feedback. Will bring up with the team for sure! How's *FreshDashDeliver*? I am really excited about that idea too."

Tino: "Good plan. Yes, we are excited too. We are spending a lot of today gathering information and insight from a few experts. We're new to the social entrepreneurship space and trying to learn the ropes a bit before we dive in head-first. In fact, I just saw Sara walk in. I better go catch up with her. Good luck, and talk to you later."

Sara spots Tino as he heads over and they meet up at an empty work station. They spend some time catching up and also mapping out ideas for the initial prototype of their food delivery service idea. Within the hour, Jay joins too.

Tino: "Okay guys. Let's catch up properly now that we're all here. Sara and Jay, what did you learn, what do we need to prioritize right now?"

Sara catches up the team on her conversation with Shonda. She talks about the various terms and how they fit under the broader term, *social innovation*. She talks to them about the role of impact and how it can literally be the feature that defines them as a social enterprise. She talks about how the U.S. doesn't have a legal definition for social enterprise, but they should be ready to speak about their impact and business model if they do adopt the term to describe their work and business. She also emphasizes the seals and certifications, noting that a number of them may apply to their work too. She recaps that the movement for social enterprise is global, reiterating that they are part of a much broader group of entrepreneurs seeking to create change through their businesses.

> *Sara:* "It was a really interesting conversation. One thing I wanted to ask you, and something that we should really think about as early co-founders, is what role we think impact has in *FreshDashDeliver.*"

> *Jay:* "Well, I don't want to speak for everyone, but for me, our company wouldn't exist without our impact goal. I mean, minus that, we would be a food delivery business. While I think it could be a profitable model, our goal seems to be to specifically benefit and deliver food to people who don't have access. Hopefully we can find ways to concretely measure impact by looking at the improved health of our clients and even the emergence of local food stores."

> *Sara:* "I agree. I really see this as an impact-first company. The day we see a consistent plateauing or decline of impact is one when we have to really reconsider our business and revenue models."

> *Tino:* "I hope it's not against my better judgment, but I tend to agree. To be honest, there are probably better options and models for making money, but what interested me about this business is how defined and clear the impact is."

> *Sara:* "Ok! That actually clears up some critical early stage things that came up from my talk with Shonda. Knowing where impact fits in and how committed we are to it not only pursuing it as a goal, but also making it a focus helps with measuring and reporting impact, which will inform

where we fit into the social enterprise spectrum. I have a feeling it might help us in figuring out a legal structure too.

"Considering how vast the global space for social enterprise is, I think it's also a good idea for us to see if other companies have tried this and what they learned in the process. If you guys don't mind, I want to take the lead on figuring out our first prototype—I have some ideas, but I think the main thing we need to figure out is whether our delivery service will be solving a pain point and be a really desirable service, or simply a 'nice to have' non-essential."

Tino: "I'm fine with that. But, I want to hear more about what Jay learned and what a legal structure might mean for our company."

Jay updates the team on his meeting with Ian. He overviews the various traditional legal structures available as well as the new *hybrid* structures that combine elements of a nonprofit and for-profit structure. He also talks about *tandem* arrangements that involve creating multiple legal forms to achieve the overarching goals of the company, such as a for-profit and nonprofit entity. He dives into aspects of one of the popular hybrid structures, the benefit corporation, including its availability in over 30 U.S. states and jurisdictions. Additionally, he explains the difference between the B corporation certification and benefit corporation legal status, and explains that companies can actually pursue both.

Jay: "So, my big question to you guys is, based on our objectives, what legal form, combination, or certifications might we want to pursue?"

Tino: "Well, here's the thing. This is a five-day hackathon. Let's get real—we probably aren't going to incorporate in that time. With the limited time, we really need to focus on what we need to make a great pitch. That all being said, I sense that we are all in it for the longer haul.

"Putting in time now and thinking about our company purpose and structure could guide our efforts over the upcoming weeks, months, and—if the startup gods will it—years! So, I've built a lot of Delaware corporations and I feel comfortable with that structure—I understand the dynamics with bringing on a Board of Directors, and I like that attorneys can really guide us based on actual examples and case law. Maybe I'm just set in my ways, but I'd opt for a C corporation and one of those seals you mentioned, like the B corp certification. Or, alternatively, we could do a C corporation and create a nonprofit entity that is dedicated to advocacy and nutrition-based education.

"Those are my thoughts. You know I'm not risk-averse—just look at me working with you millennials on launching a company! But I know how many unknowns are involved in starting a company—including things like getting funding and getting our intellectual property in order. I don't know if adding these extra layers of reporting and uncertainty are good at this early stage."

Sara: "Tino, those are great points. They make a lot of sense. I just think that we have the opportunity to build our business in a different, and hopefully better way from the start with some of these new structures. We have seen how a business' goals and operations shift when companies become huge—it seems like we have a chance to build something a bit better right from the beginning.

"To be honest, I was thinking of the benefit corporation and the B corp certification, and maybe Cradle-to-Cradle if we qualify. That way, we could not only have the legal form, but we would also be part of the public-facing global community. Jay—after meeting Ian, what do you think?"

Jay: "Wow, ok. So, I think one of the most democratic and equitable forms is worker-owned cooperatives. Not only does it give each of us a vote, but any employees we have become owner-voters too. It's impactful in its own way for sure! And, Sara, as you mapped out—it's a popular global choice too.

"But, I understand that Tino and you are both thinking of a corporate form—and honestly, if we are pursuing outside funding, that may make a lot of sense. The other thing, Tino, about one of the hybrid forms is that they can protect our company in case we ever have an exit like an acquisition. It all seems far away now, but it might be a lot easier to think about a new legal structure early when we just have a few people on board rather than once our company is bigger.

"What I'm not too sure about is the idea of doing both. It seems a bit overboard to me, considering that if we pursue a legal structure—in what way more do you need show the commitment to impact? Anyway, those are my thoughts. Hopefully we have enough to map out a strategy we can talk with an attorney about!"

They take a break to think through a few of the discussion points. Sara researches more aspects about the legal structures online. Jay looks over his notes from the meeting with Ian. Tino takes a walk around the block. When they get back, they are ready to move along the conversation.

Tino: "Okay guys, I'm in. Let's think about the benefit corporation. I like that it has some broader recognition in other states too. And I like that it can really send a clear message about how we align with impact and the integral role social impact plays for us. I might suggest, though, that we opt for the certification too. If we recertify every two years and we are a new company, the cost shouldn't be enormous, and it could help us get to our right clients, funders, and supporters sooner."

Jay: "Awesome! Wow, if *FreshDashDeliver* makes it big one day, we'll remember this conversation. How cool. Okay, let me spend some time finding an attorney who can help us make this happen. I know this isn't mission critical for our pitch on Saturday, but if we are looking past this week, it will help to get the ball rolling!"

Sara: "Cool. Okay guys, it's already 4pm. I'm going to stay here and map out prototyping ideas."

Jay: "Yeah, I'll stay, too, to help out with that. I'll also see if I can reach out to Ian or an attorney he recommends about setting up a meeting to discuss our formation."

Tino: "I'm meeting my friend Rosa to figure out how the heck social enterprises get funding to scale and grow. I'll catch you guys up tomorrow morning. See you back at IMPACTATHON bright and early."

Tino makes his way over to Menlo Park—a nearby city known for its density of venture capital firms—to speak to a friend of his, Rosa Lee. She has recently launched an impact venture fund and he thinks she will be a perfect person to speak to about fundraising.

When Rosa was in grade school, she learned that the Amazon River has more tributaries than any other river. Since then, she affectionately refers to herself as an "Amazon River

American". Just like her namesake, she considers her pan-ethnic heritage—including Irish, Brazilian, Afghani, Vietnamese, and South African lineage—as tributaries to her identity as an American. Growing up in a small town outside of Portland, her nickname helped when people asked the sometimes-welcome, sometimes-dreaded question, "So, where are you from?"

After her schooling and college in and around the Pacific Northwest, Rosa graduated with a finance degree and then worked on Wall Street before moving to Colorado to launch a startup company. The company did well and had a successful exit after six years. Rosa then took up an open offer to join a venture firm in Silicon Valley. She managed a portfolio of companies, made investments in early-stage companies, and saw huge failures as well as some exceptional successes. With a deep passion for conservation, she decided to take a leap after a few years to launch her own social enterprise in the space. While her company had some strong initial traction, it end-ed up not being sustainable, and they had to close their doors within two years, after they couldn't raise enough funding to expand their operations.

Through her experience, Rosa saw a huge need for better funding options for impact-driven companies. It led her to co-found a fund focused on social impact. Their fund invests in early-stage social enterprises and seeks a return of both invest-ment and impact.

> *Tino:* Hi, Rosa! Thanks for meeting up. I'm working with a few co-founders to launch a social enterprise.

> *Rosa:* Tino, it's great to see you. I was keeping up with your blog from your Peace Corps trip. Sounds like it was an amazing experience. So, tell me a bit more about your new venture and how I can help.

> *Tino:* Thanks for reading—and for your comments. It was

pretty incredible. It paved the way for this new company. So, our mission is to deliver fresh, healthy food to underserved areas, focusing on urban poor.

We are leaning toward incorporating as a benefit corporation and are also considering pursuing seals and certifications such as B corps to show our commitment.

We are also looking for initial funding to form a small team to create recipes, cook, package, and deliver food offerings to a focused test market. I heard you speak on a panel a few weeks back about funding for companies in the social impact sector. It seems like your experience and perspective could be really helpful to us right now as we map out our strategy.

Rosa: Funding social enterprises is something I can talk all day about! I've seen it from both sides, as a social entrepreneur and as a funder. I'm happy to help. Feel free to ask me anything.

24 HOW DOES FUNDRAISING FOR SOCIAL ENTERPRISES DIFFER FROM FUNDRAISING FOR OTHER KINDS OF STARTUP COMPANIES?

Well, if you are comparing social enterprises to technology startups, there can be some differences. A lot of tech startups pursue, or aspire to pursue, venture capital. Venture capitalists provide funding on a debt or equity basis. Basically, they make money when their startups make money. They want a return on their investment, so they are looking for big market opportunities. That's why tech startups are often a good fit for venture capital—because they can often scale more easily and are better-poised to grab a substantial share of a given market.

For social impact companies, however, there is a focus not

only on monetary progress but also on impact. How that translates for an investor is in a difference in the way investors engage with social enterprises, which can be summed up as "less, shorter, and fewer."

Let me explain:

1. **Less investment.** The potential total growth and scaling potential of social enterprises today tends to be smaller, so investors tend to invest less seed capital in social enterprises than in more traditional companies, especially tech companies.

2. **Shorter funding.** The longevity of investors tends to be more limited with social enterprises. A venture capitalist who invests in a Series A (initial round) of funding of a scalable tech company will often stick around and invest in subsequent rounds (i.e., B, C, etc.) too. For a social enterprise, it often happens that the funding raised in the initial investment often represents 90% of the total investment that will be made to that social enterprise from that particular investor.

3. **Fewer traditional firms invest in social enterprises.** Now, this actually cuts both ways. Currently, fewer traditional investment firms regularly invest in social impact companies. That being said, considering the growth of the market of the impact sector, having a few social impact companies in a venture fund's portfolio could be seen as desirable for that fund. So the growth in the whole social enterprise sector could open up avenues for traditional investment funds to consider funding social enterprises in the future. A big exit for a social enterprise would, of course, really blow the space wide open too.

Tino: Wow, okay. I've always been part of that hot, new startup with latest greatest technology. We've walked into investment meetings with barely a working prototype and received $1 million to build and scale without a lot of questions asked. I sensed that this would be a different path—but it seems like a pretty uphill climb.

Rosa: I think I remember the company you're talking about; you guys did pretty well there too, if I remember correctly. You're right that it's different—but it is important to work smarter and not just harder when you are a social enterprise. There are some unique opportunities to fundraise that can be a good fit for social entrepreneurs.

Tino: That's what I want to know—

25 HOW CAN SOCIAL ENTERPRISES RAISE FUNDS?

Yes, that's a critical question. The first thing you need to decide is whether you'll be a nonprofit or for-profit enterprise.

You likely know that nonprofit organizations can be social enterprises, too. This usually means that they have a business model, are generating revenues, and are at least partially sustainable. Nonprofits that are charities often receive the majority of their operating budget through donations and foundations and aren't generally considered to be social enterprises. Initially deciding whether you are a for-profit or nonprofit is critical in knowing which kinds of funding sources are available.

Funding sources for nonprofits

Grant Space (www.grantspace.org), a useful online resource

from the Foundation Center, outlines the following funding sources for nonprofit social enterprises[83]:

- Fees for goods and/or services

- Individual donations and major gifts

- Bequests

- Corporate contributions

- Foundation grants

- Government grants and contracts

- Interest from investments

- Loans/program-related investments (PRIs)

- Tax revenue

- Membership dues and fees

- Sales

Funding for for-profit social enterprises

But what if you are *not* a nonprofit? What if you are an entrepreneur launching a for-profit social impact startup? Your options are a bit different. Namely, you can look to:

- Friends and family

- Crowdfunding for donation

- Crowdfunding for investment

- Impact investors

- Small business loans

- Awards/prizes from hackathons, contests, pitch events

---

83 http://grantspace.org/tools/knowledge-base/Funding-Resources/General/How-are-nonprofits-funded

- Foundation investment through program-related investments (PRIs)

- Sales

You can choose to form either a nonprofit or for-profit. Whichever one you choose fundamentally defines how you will raise funds.

Social entrepreneurs may soon begin to notice that the distinction between for-profit and nonprofit organizations is becoming blurred. One thing remains certain, however. The ideal seed money always comes from people with the ability to invest more at a later time. People who donate $25 are likely to donate again, while people who donate $4 million are less likely to.

> *Tino:* Totally agree on that last point. It's the same for volunteering too. If you get someone to volunteer with a cause, there's a stronger likelihood they might donate. Okay, I've heard a ton about crowdfunding, let's just get the basics straight...

26 WHAT IS CROWDFUNDING FOR DONATION?

Ah, crowdfunding. Can you believe a decade ago it wasn't even a word? Luckily it is exactly what it sounds like, raising funds from a group, or crowd. What's been incredible about seeing the massive growth of crowdfunding and crowdfunding platforms is to see how it also democratizes fundraising in a unique way.

Crowdfunding for donation (aka perks-based, donation-based crowdfunding) is where it all started. Let's look at some of the key features, pros, and cons to understand it better.

Crowdfunding for Donation

Key Features:

- Anyone can provide funding for a campaign

- The contribution is a "donation," often rewarded with perks or benefits—but not equity

- There is no financial return for contributors

The Pros:

- It's the easiest form of crowdfunding to set up (i.e. no legal requirements)

- Anyone can contribute from anywhere

- There is no limit to the number of funders or amount of funding requested

- You can make a direct appeal to customers, friends, and family for small to mid-range amounts

- Social entrepreneurs can deliver value through non-monetary perks (i.e. they can find ways to create value for the funder, without a prohibitive cost to the social enterprise)

- You can build community, marketing, and branding in addition to raising funds

- It can serve as a way to test out an idea, concept, features, or pricing by getting customer feedback through interaction with the campaign, comments, orders, etc.

- You can validate the concept and attract other forms of funding (i.e., venture capital, impact investment, angel funding, friends and family, etc.)

The Cons:

- Though not often the case for social entrepreneurs, crowdfunding can create backlash for businesses—a for-profit business asking for donations can raise eyebrows

- It can be time-consuming and resource-intensive, especially for larger funding goals and can require a substantial marketing budget, high touch points for those launching, and involvement on various social media platforms and engagement tools

- It is based solely on goodwill, so if the project changes significantly or doesn't end up materializing, it may mean reaching out to numerous stakeholders to inform and potentially refund them

- Some platforms require raising all requested funds within a certain time frame, or none of the funds are released

- The platform itself will take a percentage of the funding raised

- Crowdfunding can be a boon for social entrepreneurs who are having trouble securing funding through more traditional routes because it can 1) raise interest, excitement, awareness about your cause and mission, 2) lead to some substantial fundraising, and 3) validate your social enterprise concept as the company pursues more funding ahead.

27 WHAT IS CROWDFUNDING FOR EQUITY?

Crowdfunding for equity (also known as "equity crowdfunding" and "investment crowdfunding") takes the same core of crowdfunding but offers a financial return. It has the potential to become one of the biggest game-changers for social enterprise fundraising!

As you'll see, new rules are being put into effect that democratize the ability for anyone in the U.S. to invest in a given startup, contingent on the startup filing the necessary documents.

Why does it matter for social enterprise? Well, it can let people vote with their dollars in a whole new way. Social enterprises who have been rejected by more traditional capital can appeal directly to their consumer and beneficiaries to gain traction, support, and funding.

A Look Back at the Legislative History of Crowdfunding for Equity

To understand this better, it makes sense to look back at the legislation that has enabled crowdfunding for equity to be an option. President Obama signed into law the JOBS Act on April 5, 2012. Title IV of the JOBS Act includes groundbreaking crowdfunding legislation[84] in that opens up investment in start-ups to anyone—not just accredited investors.[85]

The Securities and Exchange Commission (SEC) has historically had strict rules around who can invest in small businesses and startups. On the whole, small private businesses seeking funding are required to register securities with state and federal governments—a process that can be pricey and time-consuming.

---

84 http://www.innov8social.com/2011/11/what-is-crowdfunding.html
85 http://www.forbes.com/sites/timothyspangler/2012/03/28/with-the-jobs-act-congress-throws-open-the-door-for-private-stock-offerings/

As a result, small private businesses were required to solicit only "accredited investors," investors with a net worth
of $1 million (excluding residence) or minimum annual earn-
ing, who the government presumed would have the financial
literacy and investment savvy to decide on potentially risky
investments. There were a few ways to try to steer clear of
compliance issues, such as Direct Public Offerings, which I can
explain more ahead; however, on the whole it was difficult for
92% of the population who didn't qualify as accredited investors to invest in private startups.[86]

Regulation A+

Though the SEC waited nearly three full years before releasing rules to enable crowdfunding for equity, it did do so on
March 25, 2015. Called Regulation A+" ("Reg A+") of Title
IV of the JOBS Act.[87] The provision—which has been called
a "mini IPO"—enables crowdfunding for equity for both accredited and non-accredited investors.[88] This includes using
online platforms to raise funds.

Regulation A+ broadens the potential investment pool
from accredited investors to "qualified investors" which include non-accredited investors. It does have some built-in
protections, however, such as a cap on the percentage a non-accredited investor can contribute. Additionally, since it is built
more like an IPO rather than early-stage investment, there is a
substantial amount of legal work and a number of financial filings that must be successfully submitted—which not only adds
considerable cost to pursuing this funding, but also takes time.
Ideal candidates are companies that have had initial success
and are seeking to scale.

---

86 http://dqydj.net/the-aspirational-class-how-many-accredited-investors-are-there-in-america/
87 http://www.sec.gov/news/pressrelease/2015-49.html
88 http://www.entrepreneur.com/article/244278

Before you bet the farm, know that non-accredited investors can invest a maximum of 10% of their net worth or annual net income.

The new Reg A+ rules are divided into two different tiers.[89] Here are a few features of each[90]:

Tier 1

- Companies in Tier 1 can raise up to $20 million
- Funds can be raised from any investor
- The SEC will review financials
- Documents must be filed for each individual state from which a company plans to accept investment

Tier 2

- Companies in Tier 2 can raise up to $50 million
- Funds can be raised from any investor
- The SEC requires audited financials (which can be costly and time-consuming)
- For Tier 2, there is also a federal pre-emption so that companies do not need to register offerings in each state in which they plan to sell securities

SEC's Rules on Equity Crowdfunding

In October 2015, the SEC also passed rules allowing non-accredited investors to contribute to online equity crowdfunding. This is for earlier stage startups seeking to raise up to $1 million in funding.

---

89 http://www.forbes.com/sites/chancebarnett/2015/03/26/infographic-sec-democratizes-equity-crowdfund-ing-with-jobs-act-title-iv/2/
90 https://www.crowdfunder.com/blog/equity-crowdfunding-infographic/title-iv-regulation-a/

Here are 5 things social entrepreneurs should know about these recently-passed rules[91]:

1. **One million dollars in 12 months.** Startups can raise up to $1M through online equity crowdfunding from unaccredited investors, in a 12-month period.

2. **5% or $2,000 for those making less than $100,000 per year.** Aspiring crowdfunding investors making less than $100,000 can commit 5% or a maximum of $2,000 toward equity crowdfunding, within one year. For the those making $100,000 or beyond, the limit is 10% or $100,000, also within a year.

3. **Newbie audit exemption.** first-time equity crowdfunding issuers are exempted from the requirement for a financial audit (costly!) prior to raising equity crowdfunding fund

4. **Raising $500,000– $1 million.** Startups looking for less than $500,000 funding in online equity crowdfunding can provide tax returns that have been "reviewed" by an independent tax accountant. This is also true for first-time equity crowdfunding companies raising between $500,000 to $1 million.

5. **Yes, there are more questions than answers.** Perhaps you have more questions? Join the club, as well as the collective crowd! The best thing to do now is to stay informed as new crowdfunding platforms appear, and existing crowdfunding platforms pivot to make room for this new way to invest. For social entrepreneurs, though there are so many questions still in the air, the big thing doesn't change: crowdfunding works best when it

---

91 Adapted from "5 Quick Things Social Entrepreneurs Should Know About SEC's New Equity Crowdfunding Rules": http://www.innov8social.com/2015/11/5-things-social-entrepreneurs-should-know-sec-equity-crowdfunding-rules

is backed by integrity. For every hardworking, mission driven social entrepreneur trying to stake a claim, there might be a few others who are "greenwashing" their way to online equity crowdfunding investment. It is important to stay above the fray and and make good choices about whether your startup is in a good position to have ROI-seeking investors, how you measure impact, and whether taking on equity-funding might hamper, impede, or otherwise negatively impact your drive and focus to create positive impact. It's an exciting time, for sure! But a few wayward examples, and this potential boon for social entrepreneurs could take turn for bust.

28 WHAT IS A DIRECT PUBLIC OFFERING?

There is also a unique crowdfunding option that can be useful to social entrepreneurs. A Direct Public Offering, also known as investment-crowdfunding or crowdfinancing, provides avenues for private companies to work within state law to raise funds—versus federal law, as companies can now do with Regulation A+.

Before the SEC passed Regulation A+, DPO's were one of the ways[92] that private companies could work within their state legal infrastructures to solicit equity investments from non-accredited investors.

With Regulation A+ in place, companies who are looking to engage in crowdfunding for equity will have to make the initial decision of whether to pursue state crowdfunding for equity through DPOs (usually smaller amounts of funding raised) or

---

92 http://www.cuttingedgecapital.com/resources-and-links/direct-public-offering/

go for the federal Regulation A+ funding (larger sums raised but also more time and documentation required).

Here are a few features of DPO's[93]:

DPO

Key Features:
- With a DPO, a private company can offer an investment opportunity to anyone
- Non-accredited investors can participate
- Investors expect a financial return

Pros
- Any type of organization or company (nonprofit, for-profit) can invest for equity. This includes hybrid legal structures like benefit corporations and social purpose corporations.
- Investors can invest directly (there is no middleman)
- A company can offer any kind of investment (e.g., equity, debt, revenue-based investment contracts, pre-sales, for perks)
- Since it is a newer form of crowdfunding for investment, social enterprises can be "first to market" in raising funds for their cause or innovation
- This could replace an angel round or Series A round (past DPOs have raised upwards of $500,000, $1.2 million, and even $2 million)[94]
- DPOs can build broader community, marketing, and branding while fundraising

93 http://www.cuttingedgecapital.com/wp-content/uploads/CEC-Crowdfunding-Chart-.pdf
94 http://www.cuttingedgecapital.com/dpofaqs/

- DPOs are like "faucets" that can be turned off and on so companies can engage in multiple rounds of funding after the initial DPO filing

Cons

- It's a newer form—fewer people know about it and even fewer are incredibly familiar with it

- It requires state registrations (which could mean more paperwork if raising funds across states) and legal formalities

- It can take 4-8 weeks for paperwork and legal compliance before launching a DPO

- Founders might need to manage relationships with numerous investors

- It is more resource-intensive and may require professional marketing and media services

Tino: I have been part of a number of companies and even invested a little. My co-founders are first-time entrepreneurs and were asking me about this, and I thought you might have a good way of explaining it...

29 WHAT IS ANGEL INVESTING? HOW DOES IT WORK?

Angel investors are those who invest at the earliest stage of a company's launch and operations. Oftentimes you can raise angel funds with charisma and a timely, powerful idea. However, if you want to raise funds beyond angel investment, you have to raise them based on concrete results and accomplishments.

To put the investor community into context, the venture capital investor market is over $22 billion annually. The angel investor market is a little smaller, but still enormous, at $20 billion annually.[95] That's a huge pool of potential investors for budding startups.

But as you may know, Tino, there is a market that eclipses both angel investors and venture capitalists: friends and family "investors." They make up a whopping $60B market![96]

The moral of the story could be to be nice to your friends and family and prove to them, beyond anyone else, that your startup idea has wings. But though the market size is massive, startups receive an average of $23,000 from friends and family.[97] While that may be enough to get started and perhaps develop a prototype in order to scale and hire talent, a company will very likely need to develop relationships with outside investors or consider alternative funding (such as crowdfunding)...or better yet, build a product or service that can generate revenue quickly!

30 WHAT IS IMPACT INVESTING? HOW IS IT SIMILAR TO AND DIFFERENT FROM VENTURE CAPITAL FUNDING?

Unlike venture capital funding, impact investing seeks more than financial return. It is generally considered to be a more socially responsible form of investing and tends to have roots in ethical—especially environmental—issues, making it a good choice for social entrepreneurs.

Impact investing is a spectrum, with a 100% grant-making charity on one end and microfinance on the other. Many impact investors embrace a multitude of points along the spectrum.

95 https://www.fundable.com/learn/resources/guides/investor-guide/types-of-investors
96 https://www.fundable.com/learn/resources/guides/investor-guide/types-of-investors
97 https://www.fundable.com/learn/resources/guides/investor-guide/types-of-investors

The problem is that impact investing can go against the double-bottom line and triple-bottom line because it may not easily allow for you to make tradeoffs. You don't actually know the financial outcome, and it can be difficult to make a decision on how to spread the funds evenly. For example, do you use $1 million to help 100,000 people, or $100,000 to help one million people?

It can be confusing. After all, it can be hard to know what your equity return will be in five years. My best advice for you is to set rules before you start your social enterprise and stick to them. Ask yourself, does your company offer a better chance to make sufficient impact or profit? If the answer is profit, then you can look to maximize the profit and create a business plan around that. Then, as long as you break even you can maximize the impact. If you instead seek to maximize impact, then you may have to keep your operations lean to properly maximize impact and then only scale operations when you can prove out your impact model.

This actually reminds me of a quote by the venture capitalist Sean Foote. He said, "An investment without a liquidity event is charity. If you are making an impact investment, then you have to believe that there will be an exit."[98]

31 WHO ARE A FEW MAJOR IMPACT INVESTORS?

The best investors are people you already know! As you launch your business and begin prototyping and getting customer feedback, it is a good idea to look closely at your networks to see if there are any investors you can approach—not only for funding, but also for some great feedback on your pitch and business model.

---

98 Foote, S. (2015, July 20). Impact Investing [Personal interview].

Finding major impact investors can be a difficult process because the impact investor space tends to be fragmented.

Here are a few major impact investors you can research further:

- Toniic http://www.toniic.com/
- Gray Ghost Ventures http://www.grayghostventures.com/
- Elevar Equity http://elevarequity.com/
- Sonen Capital http://www.sonencapital.com/
- Lok Capital http://lokcapital.com/
- Bamboo Finance http://www.bamboofinance.com/

Tino: Thank you, Rosa. This has been immensely helpful!

Rosa: Tino, I am happy to help. There is one meeting I might suggest all three of your co-founders attend. I can introduce you to George. He is a dear friend of mine and an expert in measuring impact. As you form and build your social enterprise, it will be important to determine how and when you will measure impact, how often, and to whom you will report it.

Tino: That sounds like an important piece of the puzzle. Thanks for the suggestion and offering to introduce us. I'm sure we would all enjoy speaking with him.

WEDNESDAY AT IMPACTATHON

Jay checks his smartphone again as he steps off the train and on to the platform. Yup, it is really 6:34 AM. He and Sara had stayed at IMPACTATHON fairly late the night before, though even as they left a few teams lingered on, seeming fully immersed in conversation or coding. As they exited the building, both of their phones simultaneously buzzed with an incoming text message from Tino.

> *Tino:* "Great meeting with Rosa. So many ideas. I'll be there at 6 tomorrow. See you."

And then a follow-up clarification.

> *Tino:* "AM."

They both laughed, with a combination of giddiness to learn about Tino's updates and exhaustion after a long and consuming day. Tino was coming early, and they had a lot of work to do before pitches on Saturday. That meant they were all going to have to be there early.

As he turns the corner toward IMPACTATHON, Jay picks up the pace. This is all getting pretty exciting.

* * *

Sara picks a tea bag from the eclectic assortment and then fills her mug with steaming water. She wanted to get to IMPACTATHON early, but had no idea that at 5:23 AM, she would be the first one here.

She's glad, though; it will give her a minute to plan the day out. Sara worked on prototype ideas a lot yesterday—both on her own, with Jay, and then a little more after she got home— and she is pretty sure that they can actually build and test out a simple version of the ideas by early afternoon. Especially with this early start.

Within half an hour, a few teams clock in and then Tino strolls over with a smile.

> *Tino:* "You got here early? That's the sign of a determined entrepreneur. We have a lot to do today."

Sara: "For sure! It's the halfway mark today, and I'm hoping we get some kind of prototype out. They said the more customer feedback, the better. I would love to be able start hearing if our idea resonates with folks, you know?"

Tino: "Yes, we must. I want to focus on mapping out a few different business models too."

Tino pulls out a few notes from his conversation with Rosa yesterday just as Jay walks over.

Jay: "Sorry guys, this is the earliest train I've ever taken over. Has Tino already given his update on yesterday's meeting?"

Tino: "Right now. So, Rosa had a lot of good information. She has been in our shoes, but in her case, the social enterprise couldn't get enough funding to scale. That's why she started this impact fund.

"In terms of key takeaways, they are: 1) We should aim for friends and family funding first. It's the most accessible funding and will avoid us going to VCs too early; 2) We should really think about doing a crowdfunding for a donation campaign. It will tell us if our startup has any mass appeal and will give us a marketing boost. The risk there is if we don't raise enough funds or can't deliver on any rewards; 3) After we kick off our work in a bigger way, we'll have to think about investment or funding sooner than later. We can start making a list of potential impact investors who care about impact and specifically focus on food-related businesses. Down the line, we can look at bigger pools of funding such as crowdfunding for equity options, but we need to prove out our work first.

"The biggest thing is this: we have to have a fantastic product. This all only works if we have something people want or need and something they are willing to pay for. We have to understand our target market ridiculously well and build something for them that is ridiculously good or makes something ridiculously easy. Agreed?"

Sara: "Ok, good to know. Tino, you can start the list of impact investors. It might even be useful in our pitch on Saturday. Rather than asking for funding, which might not be likely if the judges come from a more non-impact mindset, our big ask can be introductions to a few related impact investors!"

Jay: "Totally agree with all of the points. I am intrigued about a crowdfunding campaign. I've donated to a few but haven't done one before. Let's talk more about that later too. We did some work on the prototype yesterday. Sara, where are we on that?"

Sara: "Yes, here are few sketches. Let me explain the work-flow. I think we should actually go to a wholesale food market this morning and make a menu for this evening and tomorrow evening. Then, let's go to a food desert—areas of Oakland are known to lack access to healthy food—and see if we can get any sign-ups. We can get supplies, cook or assemble the food, and then deliver this evening. Then, we can get signups for tomorrow. It will help prove out the model of delivering healthy food. What do you think?"

Jay: "Yes! I think we should make the value of our meals high—because they require a lot of known and unknown costs—like the price of food, delivery, etc.; but, I think we should make tonight's meal free and then charge a subsidized rate tomorrow. I think some people may try it if it's free, but the people that find value and are willing to pay will give us a better idea of our customers."

Tino: "This brings us to a business model. And I think our business model will actually be our differentiator. I really like what Shonda mentioned about Aravind in India. They don't turn anyone away. They have built a model around quantity and excellence. I think we should actually look to target two markets—both are paying, but scaled based on what they can afford. We should offer two prices for the same meal—a higher one if you want to pay it forward and help pay for a meal to someone who might be having a hard time affording it."

Sara: "Yes! Love that. Kind of like a take on TOMS too. Buy one, give one. I wonder if we can also partner with food banks and maybe help deliver food while we are making our food deliveries."

Jay: "This works. But I think there are a few things we don't know—and we won't know until we try. For example, what if people want prepared meals or don't want prepared meals? We don't know which yet. Also, what if people don't want to purchase meal plans in advance but just want an option to decide without planning? We don't know that yet, either. We also don't know if having two or more prices for the meal will add a layer of confusion versus having a set price or value of the meal and subsidizing or discounting from there. We won't know until we try it. Let's do it!"

They come up with a plan for the next two days. The trio will head to the wholesale market, use Sara's nutrition knowledge and their smartphones to decide on simple, easy-to-prepare foods using local produce that is in season and affordably priced. Jay will stay at the market to purchase the food they need once orders are placed and will also continue working on the slides, while Tino and Sarah split forces to get signups for the food delivery. Tino will target some of the affluent areas in San Francisco near successful startup companies, where he will test whether busy employees might appreciate the convenience of healthy food delivered to their homes with the added benefit of paying it forward to cover meals for people in need.

Sara will do the same, but will target a few neighborhoods in Oakland that she knows are situated in food desert types of settings, with only fast food franchises nearby and the closest fresh food purchasing options are more than two bus stops away. She, like Tino, will offer two pricing options and will also convey that if neither option is affordable, *FreshDashDeliver* can provide meals for absolutely free. She will tell them that their ultimate goal is deliver healthy food, the payment motivation comes after that.

With their game plan in place, they move to action. They spend the rest of Wednesday and all of Thursday implementing the plan.

* * *

THURSDAY AT IMPACTATHON

It's 10:28 PM on Thursday and a thoroughly exhausted Sara, Jay, and Tino are sitting at a twenty-four hour pizzeria a few blocks from IMPACTATHON. They are joined by their designated mentor at IMPACTATHON, Layla, as they wait for their order. The past forty-eight hours have been a whirlwind of activity, and this is literally the first time the three of them have had a chance to sit together long enough to debrief.

Layla has mentored at several IMPACTATHONs and likes to join teams in the last day or two leading up to Pitch Night. She thinks her feedback and insight can be more useful once teams have had a chance to build, test, and learn from engaging with their idea. As a successful IMPACTATHON alumnus, she also feels great empathy for the founders and knows how exhausted they are at this late stage in the experience. She has found that encouraging words from someone who has been in their shoes can do wonders for morale to get through the last miles of the marathon week.

The waiter comes by with their order and glances at the three co-founders who are deep in their own thoughts and then glances at Layla with a raised eyebrow. She gives him a reassuring nod as he mounts their piping hot order on a raised stand in the middle of the table and leaves them a pitcher of ice water.

> *Layla*: "I know about the basics of *FreshDashDeliver* and heard a little about your current prototyping process and market research. I'm excited to join you guys tonight and hear how the past few days have gone."

> *Sara*: "Thanks for coming along, Layla—it's so great to sit down with someone who can relate and hopefully give us a few pointers. I can't believe we made it to Thursday night. Cheers, guys, it's been a crazy couple of days! I know we're tired, but tomorrow's the last day before our final pitches. Let's catch up and update Layla—I can start.

> "Here are my updates: the wholesale market turned out to be a bit different than expected. Turns out, if you don't put in an order by mid-morning, all bets are off. Since we put in our order super late yesterday, it was more expensive than planned. We definitely wouldn't have known that if we didn't try.

> "Also, getting orders and feedback from potential customers was another adventure. When I went to Oakland to explain our delivery program and get sign-ups, to be honest, I had the door shut in my face at least a few dozen times. No kidding! Someone, thought I was running for office—and I'm not sure I won that vote, either!

"Then, after about the thirtieth person I talked to, I got a huge lucky break. I knocked on the door of a woman named Yolanda. She is a retired nurse who is super into gardening and has tried starting a community garden multiple times. She was so excited about what we are doing. It turns out, Yolanda knows all about food deserts and has even written letters to major grocery chains to find out why they won't open retail stores nearby. She signed up right away and then literally walked me over to five of her neighbors and had them sign up too. A couple of them suggested a few of their friends or family members that would be interested. Yolanda even left a message for her friend, who is a teacher at a nearby middle school, telling her to call me. She said that if this was useful and if it was good for kids and easy for parents, word would travel at a lightning speed.

"Of course, I didn't mention that lightning speed might be way too fast for us right now. But I did manage to say that we are doing a test rollout with a limited number of orders this week and that anyone else can be added to a waitlist.

"When I called the order in to Jay, we decided on cold foods so we wouldn't need to find a commercial kitchen. We went with a kale salad and hummus and chicken, or hummus and eggplant wrap for Wednesday. The wraps could be popped in the oven in case families want a hot meal."

Tino: "Ah, so that was the original plan. Boy did that change from Wednesday to Thursday.

"On my end, I wanted to hang out at a local high-traffic grocery store in downtown San Francisco. I wanted to find out if this idea had any legs with customers. I tried to catch people right during a lunch break when people dropped by for things like sandwiches in the readymade food section. I figured these might be right in our target—folks that value (and are willing to pay for) the convenience of freshly prepared, easy to find meals.

But, in the process a few unexpected things happened. One was that I was nearly kicked out of the store. An employee spotted me and then told me I was on private property and that there was a strict no solicitation policy. I was upset because at that point I was just talking with people and wasn't even directly selling anything or even getting signups. I wanted to see if I could validate the problem first. I almost left, too, but then hung around for a bit after the employee left the area.

"The second thing was that I walked up to a man who was deciding on a readymade sandwich and talked to him. He was curious about what we are doing. He asked me a lot of questions—many more than I asked! It turns out that he is an executive at that grocery franchise. He was visiting from the store's headquarters and was doing some fieldwork at the store to research the growing market for ready to eat foods at that location.

"It would be an understatement to say he was intrigued by what we are doing. He said that the challenge with readymade foods is that they have a short shelf life, and that can mean that lots of food is wasted. It gave me an idea: what if stores like his could donate or sell us their unused prepared foods and we could distribute right away? It would divert waste and help get good food to people who could benefit immediately."

Jay: "Ah, okay, so that's why you called us with no signups—I thought maybe it was a product-fit issue! Well, when Sara got back, I had just started buying produce from the wholesale food market and we headed back to IMPACTATHON to wash everything, prepare the salads and wraps, package it all, and then get on the road so we could deliver the meals in time.

"I don't know how, but we pulled it together and somehow served 12 meals, mostly for individuals but to a handful of families too. Luckily, the locations were all near each other—all in Oakland—and we delivered the last meal a little after 7:30 PM. It was nuts but so incredibly rewarding to see how happy everyone was to get their deliveries. A few had visible health problems, and others said that without our *FreshDashDeliver* meal, they would have opted for canned food, leftovers, or maybe gone to one of the local fast food spots."

Sara: "Right, so that was Wednesday. We actually had 14 signups, but one person didn't end up wanting the delivery and one wasn't home and we didn't want to leave it outside their door. On a side note, it made me think that if we scale up operations here, there might be a food waste situation for us too. I guess we'll have to just keep that in mind ahead.

"The good news in all of this was that 11 people signed up for a Thursday meal too; that's over 90%! And best of all, close to 60% opted for the subsidized plan. It seemed people *wanted* to pay something for it. Another note for us, a few people asked if they could use food stamps toward the deliveries. That's something we can look into ahead too."

Tino: "Wow, really good work on Wednesday, team."

Sara: "Seriously, guys! I can't believe we pulled it off. Of course, Thursday was a completely different ballgame."

Tino: "Yes, Thursday. That's when I talked to my new friend Charles from the grocery store headquarters. It turns out, he wanted to test something too. He said he would sell us food that was good but that would expire soon at a very discounted rate for Thursday if we delivered it to people without access to grocery outlets. He said that if this trial worked, maybe we could talk to them about something longer-term. He thought an arrangement like this could align well with a few of their CSR initiatives too. He also shared that his family grew up on food stamps, so this was personally an issue that was very close to him.

"What we wouldn't know until late that night is exactly how many meals they would be able to donate. On a side note, that could be a challenge with a model like this— there is a natural flux in supply and demand.

"Anyway, Charles called me late on Wednesday and said they could donate 30 meals. Good news, right? Well, kind of. The food would cover the Oakland orders, but I hadn't gotten any signups from San Francisco. We didn't really know if a 'pay it forward' model would work in food delivery.

"So, I texted you two."

Jay: "Right, that was the one at 11:52PM on Wednesday if I remember correctly! There wasn't much we could do then, but we all did post all over our social media. I created an online form and we sent it out to our friends and colleagues on our personal and professional profiles. And then, we let the Internet work while we tried to catch some sleep.

"It kind of worked. We woke up with about seven orders from the San Francisco area for people who would pay a premium to have food delivered directly to their work or home at dinnertime, knowing that their order would help pay for a donated or subsidized meal too.

"It was a relief not to have to go to the wholesale food market early on Thursday, since the food orders were in place, and we could just focus on filling the rest of the orders. Tino, I think you swung by the grocery store early on Thursday to pick up the food, right? By late morning, I saw that we had a few more hits on our online form. We were up to a total of nine sign-ups, and the exciting thing was that nearly all opted for the pay it forward model!"

Sara: "Right, so we met up late morning at IMPACTATHON, with the food and about 20 orders to fill. The thing is—and this is an important thing to note—the food that was donated wasn't actually the most nutritious. Quick eats like macaroni and cheese and fried chicken taste good and satisfy the need for a meal on the fly, but I don't think it is a significant improvement in nutrition. This was an issue because it didn't align with our mission—our reason for starting our company.

"So, we had to think on our toes. I went back to the wholesale food market. I talked to the woman we purchased the Wednesday produce from. I gave her a super short version of our pitch. She was interested but not enough to get involved or offer any support. I bet they get random requests like ours all of the time. To be honest, though, I think that as we really launch this thing and go back and purchase from her regularly, we could build a relationship with her. She seems pretty knowledgeable about local produce, nearby farms, and the costs of different produce. She could even be a great advisor for us ahead.

"Anyway, I bought enough local produce to supplement or 're-design' the donated food. We spent the better part of the early afternoon building salads and then turning the existing food into healthier versions by adding leafy greens, vegetables, and nutritious seeds and creating a modern take on "cabbage and quinoa wraps" by using the mac and cheese as part of a "stuffing" in broad layers of romaine lettuce sheath and flatbread. It all turned out pretty well and looked nice, tasty and even artistic too."

Jay: "Right, so after we finished there and loaded the car up, Tino and I made the deliveries and collected payments. After two days 'in business', we took in just under $80 for 15 full-price or subsidized orders and delivered to 12 people or families on Wednesday and another 20 on Thursday, for a total of just over 40 meals served in two days. That's pretty awesome."

Layla: "Wow, guys. So amazing. I am speaking pretty honestly when I say that most teams do not dive as deep with their prototyping as you three have. That's a lot of work for a lean team. You should be proud. My thoughts are to start shifting your focus now from producing and creating to reflecting and analyzing. You may not realize it fully, but you have gathered a ton of valuable data points in the past two days. It's time to synthesize that data and content and think about telling an amazing story with your experience, what worked and didn't, and finding ways to cite just the right amount of data to back up your experience."

Tino: "Wow, Layla, that is very helpful. I think it's exactly what we needed to hear. And perfect timing for our next meeting. Hey, guys, don't forget, we have the meeting with George tomorrow morning. It's going to help us understand concepts around measuring impact. And like Layla said, it will be good because we have a few things to measure now."

They look up and all spontaneously clink glasses again. It's been a crazy two days of building a prototype and getting feedback and learning about the challenges and opportunities along the way, and the adventure continues.

CHAPTER 5

Measuring Impact

SARA, JAY, AND TINO MEET George outside a cafe near the train station early Friday morning in San Francisco.

George has a unique perspective on the social enterprise space. He is a third-generation Oklahoman who grew up just miles from where his grandparents were born, and who actually considers himself an honorary Nova Scotian. His family moved to Halifax during his high school years, and he discovered a love for the ocean and sailing there. He took his interest to the next level by enrolling in Semester at Sea during college. In that program, he and nearly 700 other students circumnavigated the globe aboard the *SS Universe*, visiting a number of ports and learning about everything from country history to culture to geography. George loved the experience and couldn't get enough of traveling. He put his dual math and journalism degrees to work through international postings with for-profit, nonprofit, and government organizations, assisting with data analysis and reporting. He jokes that he was part of the "gig economy" before it became a buzzword—and he has built a multi-decade career around consulting assignments that have enabled him to work from virtually anywhere. Over the course of his numerous engagements, he has become fascinated with the intersection of social impact and metrics.

George has written a number of articles on different approaches to measuring impact for highly-regarded academic journals in the space.

Tino: Thank you for meeting with us, George. We don't know much about measuring impact, but we realize that as a social enterprise and benefit corporation, this will be important for us to measure and track from the start.

George: You aren't alone! I have worked with many companies and nonprofits who either don't know much about impact measurement or struggle with which metrics to measure. I am glad we are meeting so early in your formation—it may help you weave impact measurement into the core of your operations and company culture. Feel free to ask me any questions.

Sara: Hi, George, I have some basic questions about impact measurement.

32 WHAT DOES IT MEAN TO MEASURE IMPACT— HOW ARE SOCIAL ENTERPRISES DOING IT NOW?

When you start digging deeper into this question, you'll see that it's as much about how companies are measuring social impact—as how they aren't!

You can think of measuring impact as a spectrum. Some social enterprises fall on the side of minimal, ad hoc measurement—not actively measuring impact, or estimating or relaying impact based on whatever data they have available. Meanwhile, other social enterprises are more deliberate about the process. They may use a rubric or assessment or even an independent third party to assess impact.

Interestingly, the rise in social impact funding is putting a much-needed focus on finding better, more effective ways of measuring social impact, for both internal decision-making and external transparency.

Social enterprises that currently measure impact often find existing methods to be time-consuming and limited to financial output metrics or inconsistent data collection. This can negatively impact the goals of a social enterprise's mission and its beneficiaries. Social enterprises and funders vary in levels of inefficiency while collecting data, measuring impact, and also empowering the groups and causes they serve.

Many of these organizations tend to use inaccurate methods of measurement that lack analytical scope. And, data often can't be shared in a format that would maximize benefit and communication.[99]

> *Jay:* Okay, got it. It makes a lot of sense to measure impact early and regularly—

33 WHAT ARE SOME OF THE ENTITIES AND PLATFORMS THAT FORMALLY MEASURE IMPACT?

On the funder side, more established impact funds have been building various approaches to measuring impact. From the program side, established and innovative nonprofits are looking to develop frameworks to improve performance.

Younger social enterprises can often find it difficult to build stronger measurement practices, usually citing data collection costs. In fact, most of the reporting today is still limited towards the top of the pyramid (at the investor level). Top-heavy reporting tends to lose significant context. At the same time, funders (including foundations and impact funds) are still trying to build a language of measurement.

---

99 Responses in this section are largely based on an interview with the co-founder of impact measurement platform, SoPact. Sheth, U. (2015, August 27). Measuring Impact [E-mail interview].

A few of the impact measurement tools and available platforms include:

- **B Impact Assessment**[100] - This online survey assesses a company's practices against dozens of industry best practices for social and environmental performance. It takes about 90 minutes to complete and companies seeking B corporation certification must score at least 80 out of 200. This assessment is designed for for-profit companies.

- **GIIRS**[101] (Global Impact Investing Rating System) - Similar to Morningstar investment ranking or S&P credit risk rating, GIIRS is a rating system that provides ratings for both companies and funds based on their social and environmental impact. It is derived from the B Impact Assessment.

- **GRI**[102] (Global Reporting Initiative) - While GRI is not actually a rating system or measurement tool on its own, it does provide a framework and guidelines to support the measurement and reporting of a company or organization's economic, environmental, social, and governance performance.

- **IRIS**[103] (Impact Reporting and Investment Standards) - IRIS is not a measurement tool on its own. Rather, it is a library of common indicators, metrics, and standards that companies and organizations in different sectors can use to assess and communicate social, environmental, and financial performance. It is managed by GIIN[104] (Global Impact Investing Network). IRIS uses some definitions and indicators from GRI.

100 http://bimpactassessment.net/
101 http://b-analytics.net/giirs-ratings
102 https://www.globalreporting.org/
103 https://iris.thegiin.org/
104 http://www.thegiin.org/

- **SASB**[105] (Sustainability Accounting Standards Board) - SASB develops and distributes sustainability accounting standards that help public corporations disclose material, decision useful information to investors. The standards are industry-specific and are available for free on the website. Publicly-traded companies can use SASB standards to understand and improve performance on sustainability factors and to comply with certain mandatory filings.

- **SoPact**[106] - SoPact is an online platform that has developed TurboMetrics, social impact accounting software that aims to serve as a "TurboTax for measuring impact". Companies and organizations can select metrics from different standards and open catalogs to customize their own impact metrics set. The platform allows the companies to share this data with partners, funders, and advisors to collect their data and input.[107]

- **Internal, Ad hoc, etc.** - The platforms and tools mentioned above provide guidelines and assessments that any company or nonprofit can use. However, they do not account for the numerous internal impact measurement tools and methodologies that have been developed, tested, and iterated over time within nonprofits, impact funds, companies, and startups. Additionally, with the requirements of certifications and designations a number of measurement tools are appearing or being developed ad hoc to meet the growing needs of impact measurement.

105 http://www.sasb.org/
106 http://www.sopact.com/
107 note: author has been an advisor to SoPact

34 HOW SHOULD A SOCIAL ENTERPRISE DECIDE ON IMPACT MEASUREMENT CRITERIA?

It is important to understand that, currently, social enterprise can't be ranked, rated, or benchmarked in the same way financial progress is. It's taken years for the global economy to develop universal ways to convey the financial *bottom line* of an institution; and there are deficiencies, regressions, and debate on how to accurately account for even that.

Moving to double or triple bottom line accounting definitely requires a thoughtful approach.

For social enterprises, it is important to demonstrate impact through core metrics (typically defined by standards such as IRIS by GIIN and many others). Measuring each metric may be straightforward for some but complex for many.

For example, if you are manufacturing and selling solar lanterns, it is a shallow impact (breadth first). In other words, if the social enterprise is selling thousands of solar lanterns, their variables are easy to define, whereas working on human services such as disability employment requires significant human intervention—making it difficult to measure outcome!

A young social enterprise looking to build a new business should avoid excuses such as cost or time when it comes to measuring impact. Instead, they should project social impact value based on five-year projected social and financial value. Projecting impact allows an entrepreneur to focus on their core impact approach.

35 HOW DO SOCIAL ENTERPRISES ACTUALLY USE IMPACT MEASUREMENT TO MAKE DECISIONS ON THEIR BUSINESS STRATEGIES AND APPROACHES?

It's tough to answer this question since social enterprises' structure and maturity vary dramatically.

For some mission-driven companies, information about impact measurement gained in applying for a certification or seal is used in company operations and decision-making. An example of this is Ben and Jerry's, which used information about impact measurement from their B corporation certification to make decisions along their supply chain. Once they were able to quantify their social impact, they sought suppliers who also shared their values.[108]

Measuring impact can help a company or organization align with entities that also share their values and commitment to impact. By doing so, an entire industry can create social impact as whole, through the collective effect of independent and incremental decisions.

In the immediate or most initial way, measuring social impact can create an independent success benchmark by which a social enterprise or entity can gauge its own progress.

Tino: I can speak from past experience when I say that it's hard enough to run a startup and make it viable—

---

108 http://www.triplepundit.com/2014/09/b-corp-certification-helps-benchmark-improve-performance/

36 DOESN'T MEASURING IMPACT MAKE IT EVEN HARDER FOR SOCIAL ENTERPRISES TO SUCCEED?

It can, but it can also set the company up for success ahead. Eventually an investor who cares about the impact you are creating is going to ask about that impact. Tracking early can help you get ready for that moment and seize the opportunity in a timely way when it arises.

> *Tino:* Thanks, George. This has been very helpful. We are all new to this, so we'll do some research and figure out a plan for measuring impact.

FRIDAY AT IMPACTATHON

It's late morning by the time they reach IMPACTATHON after meeting George. The place is buzzing! All of the teams, about a dozen of them, are on site putting finishing touches on their presentations, iterating their prototypes, or practicing their pitches. The teams have all come a long way since Monday—with a few having functional basic smartphone app interfaces and others having completely iterated their idea based on customer feedback.

D.Litter created a mock rewards-based litter program in conjunction with an afterschool program—it was an interesting online to offline experiment which gave them really valuable feedback of what motivates kids to pick up litter. The team of engineers then integrated a few of the key takeaways they learned with the kids into their app.

The FindNiño team, which was focusing on deploying drones to find missing children, faced a few challenges in programming software to guide the drones. They had reached out to law enforcement agencies, neighborhood watch teams, and parent associations to better understand the problem and need and to see how advanced drone technology could facilitate an effective solution. The feedback and conversations were critical but had proven challenging to schedule within a week's time. However, meeting a few startups in the drone space opened their eyes to the incredible possibility and potential growth of their idea.

Tapped, the team building a tool to allow for the reporting of excessive water use, had made progress with a prototype but were facing challenges on how to make this a sustainable endeavor. Conservation, they were learning, is a hard space to monetize. They were considering ways to make a few aspects of their tool open source so other developers and companies could more easily engage. Maybe from the data collected across all usage, they could create valuable white papers and research documents that could be sold to cities and corporations.

For *FreshDashDeliver*, the team knew so much more about their business idea, a potential business model, and opportunities to partner and scale than they had just a few days ago. Today would be the key time to synthesize everything they learned into the remaining slides for their presentation on Saturday.

> *Jay:* "Ok guys, let's do this. I propose we grab coffee and tea and sit here until we have a draft of the rest of our slides. Then we can spend the evening practicing our pitches. Sound good?"
>
> *Tino:* "Yes."
>
> *Sara:* "It's our sprint to the finish!"

Jay notes the main points on each slide, all of which will be formatted before Saturday's pitch.

Slide 4: Defining What Makes Their Solution Unique— What is the Secret Sauce?

After the recent few days of conversations with experts in the field and their adventures in prototyping, the team believes the "pay what you can" model and potential hybrid legal structure as a benefit corporation will make their food delivery business unique. They have the opportunity to combat both hunger and poor health, while also supporting locally-grown food and perhaps utilizing food that might otherwise be wasted.

Slide 5: Identifying a Business Model— How will they Make Money and Impact?

From the numerous discussions both within the team and with experts, Sara, Jay, and Tino are committed to making impact integral to the business model. The model of offering their service at two price points would enable the core service to remain the same while also ensuring affordability and access to their service.

Seeing the success of models such as TOMS and Aravind Eye Care gives the team hope that this model can, not only be sustainable and profitable but can also inherently maximize impact as it scales and grows.

Slide 6: Go-to-Market— How Will they Sell and Deliver Their Food Delivery Service?

The team acknowledges that the two markets they are initially targeting are different in many ways—i.e., the market of potential users who lack access to fresh, healthy food and those who can afford to pay it forward and might use

FreshDashDeliver for the convenience it provides and the good it does. The key will be a great product and an effective outreach campaign. They can collect orders and sales through creative campaigns on social media and online ads and can even consider partnering with existing delivery apps or creating their own platform to capture sales and improve delivery and tracking.

Though in the immediate future they plan to handle the deliveries so they can continue to learn about their customers and the existing pain points—very soon they will have to scale the delivery. The team throws around ideas such as leveraging the existing and growing network of crowdshare car services. Is there a way they could work with those companies to create a win-win scenario? It's something to consider.

Alternatively, as the food truck phenomenon has been growing, eventually *FreshDashDeliver* could focus on creating bright, recognizable food trucks equipped with fresh food and refrigeration and could mimic the "ice cream truck" model of traveling through neighborhoods stopping to deliver fresh produce wherever called upon.

Based on feedback on their prototype, there could be a viable model with any one of the ideas or a combination of a few of them.

Slide 7: Who Is Their Competition? What Sets Them Apart?

Food delivery is not new, and all three co-founders acknowledge that. However, the social impact focus is unique, as is delivery of non-restaurant food to underserved areas. As they build the brand and ethos of the company, they think there might a very positive value of being associated with delivering good. Additionally, if their meals, packaging, consistency, and delivery times become excellent, they will be innovating in a space where there may not be direct competition.

An absence of direct competitors could allow *FreshDashDeliver* to partner with nonprofits such as food banks, which are vital in the space, as well as for-profit startups such as delivery companies, which have existing infrastructures of cars and transport to ensure speedy delivery.

Slide 8: Who Is On the Team? Why are they a Winning Combination?

The unique profiles, backgrounds, and personal stories of Sara, Jay, and Tino make for a team that is diverse in age, background, and experience. The thread that ties them together is their innate desires to create a company that is mission-driven as well as profit-driven.

Jay wants to make sure to highlight Tino's experience in entrepreneurship, Sara's growing expertise in nutrition, and his own knowledge and curiosity in legal and policy considerations related to their company.

Slide 9: Financial Projections—What will Sales Be in 6 months? In 2 Years?

Tino has some strong thoughts on the financial projections.

> *Tino:* "You know, we aren't going to be profitable for awhile. Look at our test this week. We got signups and orders, but ended ultimately in giving away the food. I mean the costs involved are really high right now."

> *Sara:* "I think you're right. Our break even is going to be down the road. For the initial few months we have to stay

focused on building a great product, getting traction, and improving our work flows and efficiencies to bring costs down. I think we have great potential of not only breaking even but making a sustainable and growing profit—if we can stick it out long enough."

Jay: "Okay, I've been putting some of our numbers in a spreadsheet. After we wrap up here, I'll work on those figures and come up with a few graphs we can use tomorrow to show a break even point ahead and then growth potential after that."

Slide 10: What Do They Need? How Will They Use the Funds?

Tino: "Ah, the ask. We really have to think about what we could potentially ask the panel for tomorrow. It's a critical part of our pitch."

Jay: "Do we know who is going to be on the panel? It would be helpful to research their backgrounds, past investments, and networks."

Sara: "Nope, I asked. They said we'll all find out at the start of pitches who the judges are. I'm thinking we should also *give* them something. Namely, our product. I have some ideas on ways to make our packaging sustainable and really memorable. We didn't get a chance to really focus on packaging in our trial this week, but I can work on it to give to our judges tomorrow. I would love for them to have a clear idea of idea who we are and what we are trying to do before asking them for anything."

Tino: "Yes, that's good. Then they might remember us later too. Okay, Jay, what else do we need?"

Jay: "That's it guys. I have been taking notes. Let me create a draft of the slides and we can go over them after dinner."

Tino: "Ok, good plan. There's something I want to do before dinner too. I messaged Charles, from the grocery store, last night. He's free to meet up this afternoon. I want to update him about what we are doing and where we are. I want to see if he might sign on to be a food supply partner with us. It would be huge. And it would be a big surprise we could announce that during our pitch."

Sara: "Wow, Tino. Fingers crossed! That would be a big validation of our work and could invite other kinds of cool partnerships!"

Each team member dives into the final open projects related to the pitch. Over the next six hours, they stay in touch mostly through text messages as Tino goes off-site for his meeting, Sara sources sustainable materials and has an online chat with a friend who is a branding expert, and Jay works on the pitch deck and meets with IMPACTATHON mentors to get advice.

As the evening closes in, it's the last big joint meal at IMPACTATHON. The organizers congratulate the teams for making it through an intense week. They announce each team and the entire room erupts in applause and support. There is a sense of camaraderie among all of the participants—and as the IMPACTATHON organizers note, the world would probably be a better place if all of the ideas became reality. They also reiterate the importance of thinking beyond the pitch.

The words and support are invigorating. Sara, Jay, and Tino are reenergized as they high-five teams and share group hugs. The energy transfers to their post-dinner pitch practice. It's their final chance to bring everything together before the big day.

SATURDAY AT IMPACTATHON: PITCH DAY

It's Pitch Day. Sara reflects on this as she walks her bike into the lobby of IMPACTATHON. What seemed like a seed of an idea just months ago when she was in Kansas now has a name, logo, team, product, and feedback. She knows that most startups don't survive the two-year mark — and the statistics are even tougher for social enterprises. But in so many ways, she knows this is exactly where she wants to be and what she wants to be doing. If *FreshDashDeliver* works, or doesn't, she wants to know. She wants to learn about why it could be a potential business model as well as the pitfalls and challenges she can't foresee.

Whatever happens in today's pitch, Sara knows she wants to continue with the startup and the team. The past week has felt both like a year and like a minute, and they have come a long way with many miles still to travel.

She unhooks her helmet and affixes it to her bike, closes her eyes, and takes a deep breath before opening the doors to IMPACTATHON.

* * *

There's a calm in the air after yesterday's frenzy. Teams are setting up and giving each other final pointers as the judges take their places, and friends, family, and members of the community file in.

Sara, Jay, and Tino decided last night that Sara would be the main pitch person. With just 8 minutes, it's a lot to cover. She will introduce Jay and Tino, Jay will speak about legal structures and certifications toward the end of the pitch, and Tino will announce results of his meeting yesterday to the crowd and judges. Jay formatted and transformed the slide deck, and it now includes images and brief video testimonials from a few of the *FreshDashDeliver* customers and beneficiaries from the past week. He also added their website and contact information to each slide to make it easy for anyone to contact them and continue the conversation after their pitch.

With a warm welcome from the IMPACTATHON organizers and introduction of the judges and teams, the pitches begin. *FreshDashDeliver* is last on the roster. Sara, Jay, and Tino watch as team members—many of whom have become friends over the past week—pitch their ideas and give updates on their progress. A few of the teams get rousing applause and cheers from the crowd.

D.Litter is an early crowd favorite, as is another team, PetsQ—a come-from-behind contender. PetsQ formed just days ago, as a result of a few members from larger teams branching off to create an idea around on-demand community-driven pet rescue.

Finally, it's down to the final pitch. Sara takes the stage and is handed a microphone from the previous presenter.

> *Sara:* "What if you took on the challenge of making a healthy meal for four. Let's say you were trying to use locally grown produce and wanted to keep the meal affordable. Now let's say the closest store selling any fresh produce is more than five miles away and you don't have a car. This is the reality of food deserts, and it is the everyday situation for more than 20 million Americans. We have come up with a dynamic solution that combines the best of technology and convenience with the urgency and need for better nutrition. We are *FreshDashDeliver* and we are committed to make it easy to serve fresh, healthy food, no matter where you live..."

Sara continues through the slides, plays the videos queued up by Jay, and walks through their experience from the past week as well as their business model.

As they get to the final few slides, Sara introduces Tino and invites him to the stage.

> *Tino:* "As Sara mentioned, and as you can see, I'm the old guy on the team. I've been an entrepreneur for longer than some of you have been alive! I know the value of relationships in business. And that's what I bring to the team. I also have something exciting to announce. We received a verbal agreement from one of the largest grocery retailers in the country to partner with us to supply unused food. It is a single-store commitment for a six-month supply to see how things go—but it will mean that we will not only prevent wastage of edible food but we will work directly with the store to ensure high nutritional value."

The crowd applauds and the judges look to each other and nod in approval.

Sara introduces Jay who then joins her on stage.

> *Jay:* "Hi, I'm Jay. I'm a law student now, but I've learned a lot—this week even—about legal structures. I am going to be the Chief Impact Officer here and will be finding creative and valuable ways for us to measure and improve our impact and ways to use storytelling to share meaningful impact stories with all of you. We are planning to incorporate in one of the new hybrid legal forms to formalize our commitment to social impact. As Sara said in one of our early meetings, we are 'impact-first,' and we never want to back down on the dual purposes of our company to serve our mission and create a profitable business. We strive to be a great example of social enterprise in California and in the

U.S. and will constantly be looking for ways to improve our triple bottom line."

The panel asks a number of questions—on the business model, long-term viability, and competition. While Sara is in mid-sentence, the timer rings as their eight minutes end.

The judges file out and head to an empty conference room so they can discuss each of the teams. There is a collective sense of relief and anticipation in the room as participants and share thoughts on the presentations, and exhale.

SIX MONTHS LATER

If five days at IMPACTATHON felt like whirlwind, the past six months have been nothing short of a sometimes-happy, sometimes-intense roller coaster!

After the teams pitched on Pitch Night, the judges deliberated for almost forty minutes—which, as was later mentioned, nearly broke a record. During that window of time, IMPACTATHON organizers surprised participants by having each select the startup idea that had the greatest "impact potential"—the team whose core idea could positively impact either the most people or could most substantially and integrally impact those who engaged. IMPACTATHON participants were asked to look beyond the pitch and prototype, and judge the underlying idea. This unexpected peer favorite vote only mounted the excitement and fueled new surges of adrenaline.

The "impact potential' voting also brought the participants together in a meaningful way. While the focus of the week was on coming up with a compelling pitch, prototyping, and presenting themselves in the best light, this was a chance to step back and look at the ideas through an impact lens. IMPACTATHONers gathered and asked each other questions. They weighed out the potential of various ideas, setting aside execution but focusing, rather, on the core concepts.

After much debate and a final secret ballot vote, the organizers of IMPACTATHON said they had a People's Choice winner.

When the judges reemerged from their deep deliberations, they were ready to reveal their selections too. The judge that was Head of Sustainability at a well-known startup announced PetsQ and D.Litter as the finalists, with an honorable mention to FindNiño. And, as it turned out, both the judges and the participants put their faith behind *FreshDashDeliver*. Judging by the comments from their peers, the idea of increasing access to healthy food not only had the potential to change the lives of those served but also to shift the market for local food options—making the impact potential high in their eyes. The partnerships and product development generated over less than a week also pointed to the potential and momentum of the idea and the impact. Additionally, though the judges had plenty of constructive criticism, they found the prototyping, deliveries, and sales promising.

FreshDashDeliver was awarded free office space for one year at the IMPACTATHON co-working space, along with $5,000 worth of software and services. In fact, each of the top teams received office space for differing lengths of time.

Being recognized by the judges, and perhaps even more so, by their peers was an incredible validation of their work and the idea behind *FreshDashDeliver*. That night Sara, Jay, and Tino toasted to the months to come and to taking every challenge and every success one day at a time.

* * *

Those days and experiences have led to a deeper exploration of social enterprise over the past six months. Sara, Jay, and

Tino know so much more about social entrepreneurship not only through their interviews and questions, but now, also through their experience.

Over the months, *FreshDashDeliver*'s operations have expanded. They hired three drivers and a handful of food specialists from the community to prepare, package, and deliver the meals. They have also partnered with two grocery retailers who not only donate food but also support the delivery and even "match" meals through donation.

These days, the three co-founders still have a lot of questions and are asked many more by the community, friends, supporters, and the company's social media fans. Most often, people want to know how they can engage in social entrepreneurship. They are looking for tangible ways to get involved and be part of the social good movement.

Armed with this question, Sara reaches out again to Shonda. Shonda visits them at their co-working space and is impressed with their work and progress, not only at IMPACTATHON, but in these months after.

> *Shonda:* "Wow, look at you all! You go! I love what you are doing here. Okay, so, Sara, you mentioned some new questions?"

> *Sara:* "Yes, we get folks asking us more and more these days about how they can create social impact. We have learned so much from our experience, but I wanted to ask you some of these questions too."

> *Shonda:* "I'm here to help. Ask whatever you like."

CHAPTER 6

Reaching Your Social Impact Potential - Taking Action

37 WHAT IS AN INFORMED CONSUMER—HOW CAN I CREATE IMPACT THROUGH WHAT I BUY?

With the shifts in the workforce and a broader shift in creative problem-solving, we are also entering the age of the informed consumer. That's someone who creates individual impact through his or her purchases and collectively can impact entire industries.

There is actually a name for this buying market,: it is Lifestyles of Health and Sustainability, also known as LOHAS. If you can believe it, LOHAS commands a $546 billion market globally!

The LOHAS market, in turn, inspires founders to launch better mission-oriented ventures and companies to more effectively pursue sustainability and impact measures.

Okay, so whether you consider yourself a card-carrying member of the LOHAS community or are just getting started with adopting the mindset of 'voting' with your purchases, there are a few concrete ways you can become a more informed consumer.

1) Check for seals and certifications

There are a growing number of seals and certifications that can denote a company's commitment to impact. We talked about these earlier. They aren't just a tool for social enterprises to stand out from the crowd; they're also a way to help all of us as consumers decide (and vote) on products and services that align with our values.

2) Check if the company has an impact report

Another thing you can do to be a more informed consumer is to check if the company has an impact report.

Many companies are becoming more active in corporate social responsibility—CSR. This can involve releasing an annual report that accounts for their impact through various measures such as charitable giving, reduction of waste, and how their sustainability decisions impact the country's supply chain.

You can check the company website and also take a look at directories such as The Global Reporting Initiative (GRI) and CSRWire.

3) Look on the company website and their social media

You can also take a closer look at the company website and social media presence. Companies are becoming more creative, vocal, and involved—not only in creating impact but also in sharing that impact with their followers and customers. Many corporate foundations are also becoming more active in how they engage in impact.

All in all, if you look at purchasing as voting, it can be empowering to think about easy ways you can create social impact through simple decisions you are already making every day.

38 WHAT IS A SOCIAL INTRAPRENEUR—HOW CAN I CREATE IMPACT THROUGH MY CAREER?

This is one of the most powerful modes of engaging in social impact. Now that you know a lot about social entrepreneurs who start mission-aligned ventures, think about social entrepreneurs who work inside corporations or organizations. These individuals have been called social *intrapreneurs.*

They operate within their company's infrastructure to ideate ways of creating impact company-wide or within their department or group. They might prototype initiatives, validate, get buy-in from key leadership, and may even scale and grow their social impact ideas—all within the company, entity, or organization. And there are a number of ways professionals can engage in social intrapreneurship.

Social intrapreneurs might be doing anything from finding ways a company can source supplies or raw materials from more sustainable sources, to working on increasing employee engagement in charitable giving, or a social intrapreneur could be redesigning the waste management within the company to try to divert more to recycling.

You might wonder, why would employees want to be social intrapreneurs?

We know that entrepreneurship is risky (over half of startups don't survive past the first year). Social intrapreneurship provides a safe space to create and ideate while still pursuing your "day job."

- Social intrapreneurship brings together employees from different departments, areas of focus, and distinct parts of the company to work on a common goal or cause. Just like your team benefitted from different voices and perspectives, social intrapreneurs can leverage talent from all facets of the company for a social cause.

- It can also create an individual sense of purpose. We spend so many hours at work, working on initiatives and projects that align with your desire to create impact can be profoundly fulfilling at a personal level, which can also leave you more satisfied with your work and role.

Additionally, social intrapreneurship can be an easy win for companies too. In 2014, Forbes wrote an article titled "2014's Most Valuable Employee: The Social Intrapreneur" [109] and said, "social intrapreneurs are quickly becoming the most valuable employees at many companies because they are good for the bottom line, good for the brand, and good for staff morale. They are being recognized as key players in tackling the world's biggest problems like poverty, hunger, and the need for universal education."

Companies committed to cultivating social intrapreneurship might also be attracting top talent, engaging existing talent in meaningful ways, and creating a collective sense of purpose and mission.

You might also be wondering *how* to engage in social intrapreneurship. Here are three things you can do right away:

- **Ask**. Ask your manager, boss, or HR representative about department-wide and company-wide opportunities to engage in social impact. Your company's internal employee website, newsletter, or bulletin board might list useful opportunities. If your company has a foundation, that might be another avenue to explore.

- **Join**. Join any work groups related to social impact, or start one! Many companies, especially large ones, feature an expansive network of 'extracurricular' activities based on employee interests. Just as you might find groups

---

109 http://www.forbes.com/sites/ashoka/2014/01/24/2014s-most-valuable-employee-the-social-intrapreneur/

related to outdoor activities, fitness training, and family activities, your company might have groups connected social intrapreneurship, sustainability, or focused on particular pressing issues.

- **Connect.** Connect with global resources such as the League of Intrapreneurs which was created by Ashoka Changemakers and Accenture in 2012.[110] It is the first network specifically for social intrapreneurs. One of its helpful resources is a "Cubicle Warriors Toolkit" for a step-by-step guide on creating social impact within your role and organization.[111] There are also a growing number of resources, videos, and publications focused on social intrapreneurship. In his TED Talk on the topic, Gib Bulloch[112] underscores the massive role intrapreneurs can play by noting that "over half of the largest economies in the world are not countries, they are multinational corporations." Finally, there is also an annual Intrapreneurship Conference[113] focused on effective methodologies and means of fostering corporate intrapreneurship.

39 I AM A STUDENT—WHERE CAN I GO TO LEARN ABOUT AND APPLY FOR FELLOWSHIP PROGRAMS FOR SOCIAL INNOVATORS?

There are literally dozens of social innovation fellowship programs, and new ones emerging regularly. Some are paid, while others are unpaid or for college credit. There are programs to meet individuals at whichever stage of life they find themselves in, whether they're in school, in an established

110 http://www.leagueofintrapreneurs.com/
111 http://www.leagueofintrapreneurs.com/toolkits
112 https://www.youtube.com/watch?v=5KYWJdU9Ltw
113 http://www.intrapreneurshipconference.com/

profession, transitioning between careers, or seeking to re-enter the workforce.

Here are few social innovation fellowship programs to research further:

- Acumen Global Fellows Program[114]
- Ashoka Fellows Program (US)[115]
- Ashoka Global Fellows[116]
- Deshpande Foundation India Fellowship Program[117]
- Echoing Green Fellowships[118]
- Greenlining Institute Fellowship Programs[119]
- Global Social Benefit Fellowship Program[120]
- Henry Crown Fellowship, the Aspen Institute[121]
- Kiva Fellowship[122]
- New Leaders Council Fellowship[123]
- StartingBloc Fellowship[124]
- TED Fellows Program[125]
- Villgro Fellowship[126]

You can also find a dynamic list of social innovation fellowship programs at Innov8social.com/tools.

114 http://acumen.org/leaders/global-fellows/
115 http://usa.ashoka.org/nominate-ashoka-fellow
116 https://www.ashoka.org/nominate
117 http://dfp.org.in/
118 http://www.echoinggreen.org/fellowship
119 http://greenlining.org/leadership-academy/programs/fellowship-program/
120 http://globalsocialbenefit.institute/education.html#fellowship
121 http://www.aspeninstitute.org/leadership-programs/henry-crown-fellowship-program
122 http://www.kiva.org/fellows
123 http://www.newleaderscouncil.org/
124 http://startingbloc.org/
125 http://www.ted.com/participate/ted-fellows-program/apply-to-be-a-ted-fellow
126 http://www.villgro.org/apply

40 I AM AN ENTREPRENEUR—WHERE CAN I GO TO LEARN ABOUT INCUBATORS, ACCELERATORS AND OTHER WAYS TO GET INVOLVED?

There are so many incredible resources in the space. Over the past few years, these tools, stories, and opportunities have also begun being compiled in one place at Innov8social.com.[127]

If you to go the "Tools" section (innov8social.com/tools) you will find hundreds of resources divided into over a dozen lists on topics such as:

- books, magazines, blogs, journals, and websites on social entrepreneurship
- academic programs and certifications for social impact
- conferences and events related to social impact
- social innovation fellowship programs and internships
- accelerator and incubator programs for social entre-preneurs

Best of all, the lists are dynamic—so you can add comments, suggest resources, and share any special insights you might have.

> *Sara:* Thank you again, Shonda! It's been exciting to be immersed in running our social enterprise, but I didn't know about a lot of these broader opportunities to engage. Definitely something we can pass on to folks when they ask us, and even look into ourselves!

> *Shonda:* My pleasure. Let's set up some time to meet with the whole team in the next few weeks. I might have a few ideas for you guys to think about and a few folks I would like to introduce you to.

---

127 As noted, the author is the founder of Innov8social

CHAPTER 7

Global Social Entrepreneurship

SARA, JAY, AND TINO MEET up most days at the upstairs office space they were awarded from the IMPACTATHON win. They also have been in close touch with the organizers and have even served as mentors for a few subsequent IMPACTATHON sessions.

Just last week, the annual IMPACTATHON Global session was announced to be taking place in three months in Kuala Lumpur, Malaysia. The event will bring together selected local teams from around the world for a three-day session. The focus there will be less on the pitch and more on building international relationships, partnerships, collaborations, and exploring ways different companies in different regions are forming their social enterprises, measuring impact, and finding funding and investment.

FreshDashDeliver has been invited to represent IMPACTATHON San Francisco, along with D.Litter and about three other social enterprises from various sessions of IMPACTATHON.

It is an opportunity to connect with a question that has come up a great deal recently for the team around global social entrepreneurship. Jay has been particularly fascinated by how the social impact sector is emerging around the world. He reaches out to Professor Zi who lectures at his university, and who regularly speaks internationally and occasionally at the United Nations.

* * *

Professor Zi invites Jay to office hours. It's a quiet Friday afternoon when they meet in Professor Zi's office at the top floor of the business building in a comfortable office with an oversized rug and shelves filled with books and curiosities from across the globe. The curios, oddities, and tomes nicely complement Dr. Zi's slightly eccentric, completely brilliant, and borderline enigmatic persona on campus.

> *Jay:* Hi, Professor. Thanks for inviting me to your office hours. I am really enjoying being part of a social enterprise and learning more about how the sector is emerging and evolving globally. Our lens into the space is based on what is happening in the U.S., specifically in California, and even more specifically, in the San Francisco Bay Area. We have the opportunity to meet dozens of global social entrepreneurs at an event in Malaysia in a few months. I am really curious about what is happening around the world in social entrepreneurship.

> *Professor Zi:* It's definitely an exciting time for social innovation in the U.S. and abroad. It's great that you are asking questions about how social enterprise is developing globally. It's easy to get so immersed in your experience that you forget to consider that everyone is facing different variables such as technology, funding, even language that could affect the way social innovation is realized and expressed. Feel free to ask me anything.

41 HOW IS SOCIAL ENTERPRISE EMERGING AND EVOLVING GLOBALLY?

It is interesting—social entrepreneurship and the ecosystems to support the sector are developing under unique circumstances, with different structures and definitions, and to address specific needs across the globe.

Let's start with an overview of a few overall trends.

1. A rapidly aging population is creating a unique need in countries such as China and Japan, which is putting a new focus on the need for sustainable solutions for healthcare and infrastructure on the horizon.

2. In other countries, it is the opposite situation. For example, countries such as Pakistan and Egypt are experiencing a "youth bulge"—where a large percentage of the population is young and will be entering the workforce ahead.

3. Countries with a strong history of cooperatives, such as Ireland and Italy, are also seeing social enterprise emerge as a close cousin.

4. Additionally and somewhat surprisingly, global "hubs" of social entrepreneurship such as India and South Africa do not yet have legal structures or defined local infrastructure for social enterprise.

5. In fact, a vast majority of countries do not have a legal structure or legal definition of social enterprise. While this is not a deal breaker for social entrepreneurs, who are anyway often marked by their tenacity, it can be a limiting factor, especially when it comes to funding and scaling.

6. Other countries have prioritized social enterprise as a force for the nation and have taken or are taking steps to build legal or government-defined infrastructures to help aid and promote the growth. The UK is a leader with multiple legal structures and a growing ecosystem of social enterprise, and Thailand, Vietnam, and South Korea also have defined social enterprise legally.

7. Another area of interest is the sheer size of the sector in various nations. While India is said to easily have the most social enterprises, estimated in the millions (including nonprofit social enterprises), countries such as Finland and Sweden have strong and growing social enterprise communities in the hundreds or thousands.

8. For some countries, the growth of social enterprise, or need for it, can be mapped to a particular date or set of events. In Japan, for example, the triple disaster on March 11, 2011 catalyzed much of what is happening in that space today. Additionally, in the Middle East, the uprisings and challenges of authoritarian power that marked the "Arab Spring" served to shed light on the need for new approaches to solving persistent societal needs, and the "Arab Winter"—a term used to explain the periods of tumult and unrest following Arab Spring— has also highlighted both the need and also the challenge of growing a social enterprise sector in areas of political and financial uncertainty.

9. There are also countries that are taking bold steps in both government structure and funding models. The U.S. has passed laws creating new categories of for-profit and for-social impact companies in over 30 states or jurisdictions. Canada, South Africa, and the United Kingdom are also taking measures to implement "social impact

bonds", which create three-way contracts between the private sector, government, and nonprofit organizations to address societal needs.

10. While it is an incredible moment for social enterprise, a few glaring challenges face the sector's global reach. Chief among them is a common language to describe and convey the impact that social enterprises make for a cause, community, and even within a national landscape. Additionally, we have yet to see any universally accepted and/or United Nations-created definitions of social enterprise. Another looming challenge is the prevalence of corruption. In certain regions it has led to the siphoning of funds from global development, which can impact social enterprise.

Jay: That is really fascinating. Maybe it's because of my own background of having family in India and living in the U.S., or just that I am really interested in how social enterprise — including any related legal structures — is evolving and emerging in the world, but I would love to dive into various regions and learn what is happening in the space.

Professor Zi: Of course! Where shall we start our global trek?

42 WHAT DOES SOCIAL ENTERPRISE LOOK LIKE IN ASIA AND EUROPE?

South Asia paints a rich and complex canvas for social enterprise. While it is the home to robust communities of social entrepreneurs, many of whom hail from around the world; the region is equally recognized for a conspicuous lack of legal and government frameworks to recognize and support the growing social enterprise infrastructure.

India, with a population of over 1.2 billion people—a third of whom are under the poverty line—is home to the largest number of social enterprises, estimated to be in the millions[128] with efforts underway to map and survey the sector comprehensively.[129] Since the country doesn't have a dedicated social enterprise legal structure, "social enterprise" includes a range of for-profit and nonprofit entities, and combinations of the two. While there has been exponential growth in the number of social enterprises emerging in South Asia, growth of the ecosystem to support these changemakers has not been as forthcoming. There are a number of challenges, chief among them being lack of funding to support growth beyond seed stage.[130] While the country is starting to see more equity financing and debt financing for growth-stage social enterprises, investors there often find a shortage of "investible enterprises which [can] provide an economic exit."[131] One trend that we see in India that we may begin to see in other hubs for social enterprise around the world is the development of more *regional* frameworks to enable growth.[132]

Pakistan has a unique profile for social enterprise, as it has one of the most proportionately young populations. Called a "youth bulge", it has the second highest percentage population of young people—with 60% of the country comprised of youth.[133] This critical mass of new voices will undoubtedly shape how social impact companies grow and scale in the country. Fundamentalist groups both threaten the advancement of social entrepreneurship through oppression and fear, but also make the case for the need for social innovation more apparent.

---

128 http://magazine.good.is/articles/is-india-really-a-hotbed-for-social-enterprise
129 http://www.odi.org/projects/2814-surveys-social-enterprise-activity-bangladesh-ghana-india-pakistan
130 India Social Enterprise Landscape Report. (2012). Asian Development Bank. Retrieved from http://adb.org/sites/default/files/pub/2012/india-social-enterprise-landscape-report.pdf
131 Jain, P. Impact Law Ventures. (2015, September 2). [Telephone interview].
132 Sonne, L., & Jamal, A. (2014). Regional Social Enterprise Ecosystems in India. Retrieved from http://okapia.co/wp-content/uploads/publications/235/India Local Ecosystem Report 2014.pdf
133 Mahar, Asiya. "Pakistan's Youth Bulge: Human Resource Development (HRD) Challenges." *IPRI.* 10 Dec. 2014. Web. http://www.ipripak.org/pakistans-youth-bulge-human-resource-development-hrd-challenges/#sthash.GXrkNtVE.dpbs

Bangladesh's evolving role in social enterprise is rooted in its leadership in space. It is home to Professor Yunus and Grameen Bank and BRAC—the largest NGO globally that employs an estimated 100,000 people.[134] These institutions, established in the 1970s, paved the way for today's small, active community of social enterprises centered in the country's capital, Dhaka, and surrounding areas. Similar to Pakistan and India, Bangladesh's government has not created any legal or financial structures to support the space.[135]

In **East and Southeast Asia**, you can find a panoply of growth and opportunity for the social impact sector—as well as growing societal and public health needs demanding innovative solutions.

South Korea was one of the first countries in Asia to define social enterprise through legislation. Passed in 2007, Article 2 of The Law on the Promotion of Social Enterprises specifies social enterprises as companies that pursue social purpose in addition to a revenue model and/or companies that reinvest profits into the business or community rather than seeking to maximize shareholder profit. The country had an estimated 1100 registered social enterprises by 2014, with a government goal of reaching 3,000 by 2017.[136]

Vietnam is another country to opt for a legal definition of social enterprise. In November 2014, over two-thirds of parliament members passed amendments to the country's Enterprise Law,[137] specifically defining a social enterprise as a business founded with the primary goal of addressing social or environmental issues and which re-invests at least 51% of its annual profits toward its social mission. Additionally, social enterpris-

134 https://en.wikipedia.org/wiki/BRAC_(NGO)
135 http://www.britishcouncil.org/society/social-enterprise/news-events/news-social-enterprise-spotlight-bangladesh-hosts-dialogue
136 Social Enterprise in South Korea: 5 Facts. (2015). Retrieved from http://www.innov8social.com/2015/01/social-enterprise-in-south-korea-5-facts
137 http://www.theguardian.com/british-council-partner-zone/2014/dec/16/approved-social-enterprise-receives-legal-status-in-vietnam

es in Vietnam can receive funds from charities, NGOs, or other enterprises.[138]

In many ways, **Thailand** is a model for leadership and ecosystem-building in social enterprise. The country has an estimated 120,000 social enterprises, which are supported by government body Thai Social Enterprise Office (TSEO). Created in 2010 to oversee the country's five-year Social Enterprises Master Plan, it has been a key facilitator in creating partner networks within Thailand and internationally and has provided critical funding to early-stage social enterprises.[139] In February 2015, the Thai Social Enterprise Promotion Act was proposed to improve the regulatory framework and tax incentives for social enterprise and promote the participation of the private sector and private capital through CSR. The bill draft was pending review as of May 2015.[140]

Inspired by its neighbor Thailand, **Malaysia** is taking major steps to include the growing space in the country's strategic planning.[141] The country does not have a legal definition for social enterprise[142]; however, Prime Minister Najib launched the Malaysian Social Enterprise Blueprint (2015-2018) to "radically transform the social enterprise sector" by increasing the country's 100 social enterprises to over a thousand within three years and building an ecosystem to help at all stages from formation to long-term growth.[143]

In **Japan**, the recent interest in and emergence of social enterprise can be linked to a specific date. On March 11, 2011, the country suffered a triple disaster with an earthquake, tsunami,

138 Smith, W. & Darko, E. (2014). Social enterprise: constraints and opportunities – evidence from Vietnam and Kenya. Retrieved from http://www.odi.org/sites/odi.org.uk/files/odi-assets/publications-opinion-files/8877.pdf
139 http://www.theguardian.com/social-enterprise-network/2012/sep/07/social-enterprise-thailand-strong-government
140 U.S. State Department report: 2015 Investment Climate Statement - Thailand . Retrieved from http://www.state.gov/e/eb/rls/othr/ics/2015/241763.htm
141 http://www.theborneopost.com/2015/07/04/a-touch-of-magic-gearing-up-for-social-entrepreneurship/
142 http://arkitrek.com/http:/arkitrek.com/the-nitty-gritty-of-social-enterprise/
143 Koas, J. (2015, May 14). PM: Foster social enterprises. The Star. Retrieved from http://www.thestar.com.my/News/Nation/2015/05/14/PM-Foster-social-enterprises-Such-entrepreneurship-vital-in-peoples-economy-says-Najib/

and meltdowns at the Fukushima Daiichi Nuclear Plant. An estimated 20,000 lives were lost, nearly a half of a million individuals had to evacuate, and the damages were estimated in the hundreds of billions USD. The events are said to have catalyzed fundamental shifts of consciousness within the country, with an increased focused on social capital.[144] In fact, a report titled "The Social Impact Investment Landscape in Japan" was submitted to the G8 Impact Investment Taskforce in July, 2014 by the Japan National Advisory Board. It takes a look at this heightened interest in social impact investing after 2011 and also addresses some of the pressing problems within the nation. Of major concern is the rapidly aging population, where by 2050 one out of three Japanese residents will be over the age of 65.[145] Young people in Japan are at the forefront of the movement for social enterprise in Japan, taking a lead in efforts to establish new operating models.[146] And though there is no standardized legal definition of social enterprise in Japan, the growth of the space can be seen through social impact training and collaboration initiatives such as the Social Innovation Forum Japan (SIFJ) and industry conferences such as the Social Issue Conference.

In the world's most populous country, **China**, social enterprise is emerging to address massive-scale issues which impact or will impact the country in the coming years. This, like in Japan, includes a rapidly aging population. The country has an estimated 200 million citizens above the age of 60—equivalent to nearly 15% of the population. And the proportion is increasing at such a pace that by 2050 an estimated one-fifth to one-third of people in China will be over 65 years old.[147]

144 Kobayashi, T. (2015, September 7). Social Entrepreneurship in Japan [Email interview].
145 The Social Impact Investment Landscape in Japan. (2014, July 1). Retrieved from http://www.socialimpactinvest-ment.org/reports/Japan%20NAB%20FINAL.pdf
146 Toivonen, T. (2012, March 31). Japanese Youth after 3.11: From Underdogs to Change-makers? Retrieved from http://www.wochikochi.jp/english/relayessay/2012/03/311haisha.php
147 How Fast is the Population Ageing in China? (2013, June 19). Retrieved from http://www.tandfonline.com/doi/ab s/10.1080/17441730.2013.797295

In fact, in October 2015 the Chinese government announced a change to the country's thirty-five year old one-child policy, to address this real concern of an aging population.[148]

The need for public and health services to serve this sector alone is an urgent call for solutions.[149] Additionally, and to give a sense of scale, it is estimated that over 80 million Chinese people comprise the nation's disability sector—and that number alone eclipses the entire populations of 90% of all countries.[150] China does not currently have a legal definition for social enterprise, and there may be some distrust in companies utilizing business models to create social impact; however, as the social enterprise sector emerges and gains momentum, one of the benefits is that there is funding available to help them scale and grow.

43 WHAT ARE THE TRENDS FOR SOCIAL ENTERPRISE IN EUROPE AND OCEANIA?

In **Europe**, the social entrepreneurship scene is growing too—a little differently.

The **United Kingdom** established the Community Interest Company (CIC) legal structure in 2005 specifically for social enterprises that intend to operate to benefit the community, rather than to benefit shareholders. It was created as a distinction from charities and has become a popular legal form for social enterprise there—with adoption by over 10,500 social enterprises. For-profit social enterprises in the UK are increasingly opting for existing legal forms such as Companies Limited by Shares (CLS), which social entrepreneurs have adopted for its simplicity, flexibility, and openness to various types and amounts of

148 http://www.bbc.com/news/world-asia-china-34697016
149 The shape of social enterprise in China. (2015, May 7). *The Guardian*. Retrieved from http://www.theguardian.com/british-council-partner-zone/2015/may/07/the-shape-of-social-enterprise-in-china
150 http://www.worldometers.info/world-population/population-by-country/

investment.[151] In September 2015, over 60 UK companies became the first in the nation to certify as B corps.[152]

Countries such as **Ireland** and **Italy**, with long histories of cooperatives, are also seeing social enterprise emerge in a unique way. In Ireland, social enterprise is being looked at as a way to rebuild the economy and create jobs. Adopting an expansive definition of social enterprise to include for-profit and nonprofit entities, the country has well over 1,400 social enterprises with hopes of growing those numbers and creating 65,000 jobs in the coming years. It has an active community of social enterprises and a volunteer-based national network called the Irish Social Enterprise Network, which addresses the growing sector and supports initiatives, such as the push for a social enterprise legal structure in the country. Ireland is also one of the few countries to have a Minister for Social Enterprise.

Italy is also a major player in social enterprise in Europe. The social cooperative, i.e., cooperatives delivering health and social services, has long been a popular legal form. The country also has a legal structure that was established in 2005 called imprese sociali for private companies engaged in social impact. Between those two forms alone, there are well over 10,000 social enterprises in Italy.[153]

France is home to the largest European social enterprise, Groupe SOS, which has 12,000 employees with an annual turnover of $1 billion USD. It benefits over one million people each year through programs addressing youth and education, workforce integration, social exclusion, and healthcare.[154] And, it is scaling in a completely unique way. Groupe SOS has sought to share its teachings and experience internationally—starting with focusing on challenges

151 Pushing Boundaries. (2014, April 1). Retrieved from https://unltd.org.uk/wp-content/uploads/2014/04/UnLtd_Research_Publication_Number71.pdf
152 Williams-Grut, O. (2015, September 24). An ethical business movement backed by Etsy, Kickstarter, and Patagonia just launched in the UK. *Business Insider.*
153 A Map of Social Enterprises and Their Eco-Systems in Europe. Country Report: Italy. (2014, October 31). Retrieved from http://ec.europa.eu/social/BlobServlet?docId=13026&langId=en
154 http://www.groupe-sos.org/en/385/about-us

in other *developed* countries. It has formed local entities and partnered with existing nonprofits in countries including South Korea
and the U.S. to develop programs to support pervasive societal
challenges.

The Nordic countries have a special connection with social
enterprise as well. Through a few examples, here we can see
the emergence of social entrepreneurship in universal welfare
countries.

Sweden, which adopted a social welfare model (called the
"Swedish Model") in the 1900s, is known for high taxation (often
nearly fifty percent for working families) which funds strong programs for education, healthcare, and family services available to
all of its residents. Since many companies and entities inherently
consider impact, Sweden provides an example of how the future
of social entrepreneurship could be, well, *entrepreneurship*. It has
approximately three hundred social enterprises which choose
from existing legal structures such as corporations, cooperatives,
trading companies, and nonprofit entities.[155]

Sweden's neighbor, **Finland**, is the only Nordic country so far to
adopt a distinct legal structure for social enterprise. In effect since
2004, The Act on Social Enterprises was passed during a time of
heightened unemployment in which disabled workers were having particular difficulty finding jobs.[156] Under the Act, a company
or entity can register as a social enterprise only if it is founded
in order to employ disabled or long-term unemployed and if at
least 30% of the company's employees fall within that category.[157]
This more narrow definition of social enterprise has led to 169
companies registering as official social enterprises there; however,
it has also inspired broader definitions of social enterprise. One
such effort led to the creation of a special seal, The Finnish Social

155 EFESEIIS Sweden National Report on social entrepreneurship. (2105, January 21). Retrieved from http://www.
fp7-efeseiis.eu/national-report-sweden/
156 http://www.ekonomiaspoleczna.pl/files/ekonomiaspoleczna.pl/public/gk/panele/Social_enterprises_in_Fin-
land_panel_E.pdf
157 https://en.wikipedia.org/wiki/Social_enterprise#In_Europe

Enterprise Mark, in 2011. This certification more broadly defines social enterprise as companies or entities formed with the primary objective of promoting social well-being.[158] Since its inception, an estimated fifty companies have achieved the seal. Under a yet broader definition (such as the EU Operational Definition which includes nonprofit entities), the country is thought to be home to over 2,500 social enterprises.[159]

In Eastern Europe, the concept and recognition of social enterprises is still developing. In the **Czech Republic**, for example, there are no specific legal structures or certifications to denote social enterprise yet, though platforms and databases such as the Thematic Network for the Development of Social Economy (TESSEA) are emerging to promote the concept of the social economy and social entrepreneurship. The number of social enterprises, including nonprofits, in the Czech Republic is estimated to be around 350.[160]

Likewise, **Romania**, is representative of its Eastern European neighbors in that, while the social impact sector is growing, the country doesn't currently have legal structures or certifications. There, however, has been a draft law proposing a legal definition of social enterprise and suggesting the creation of a new department to oversee policy and legislation related to the social economy.[161]

Oceania, comprising New Zealand and Australia, is a meaningful participant in social enterprise as well. A number of initiatives and accelerator programs have emerged. And though neither country has a dedicated legal structure, there is discussion around a model paralleling the benefit corporation model.

---

158 A map of social enterprises and their eco-systems in Europe, Country Report: Finland. (2014, October 31). Retrieved from http://ec.europa.eu/social/BlobServlet?docId=13102&langId=en
159 A map of social enterprises and their eco-systems in Europe, Country Report: Finland. (2014, October 31). Retrieved from http://ec.europa.eu/social/BlobServlet?docId=13102&langId=en
160 Map of Social Enterprises and Their Ecosystems in Europe. Country Report: Czech Republic. October 2014. Retrieved from http://i8s.us/EUreport_CzechRepublic
161 Map of Social Enterprises and Their Ecosystems in Europe. Country Report: Romania. October 2014. Retrieved from http://i8s.us/EUreport_Romania

Australia's social enterprise sector is vibrant and expanding with new resources, awards and recognition, and research. One periodic study is the Finding Australia's Social Enterprise Sector report series. Authored by a two-decade veteran social innovator and professor in Australia, Dr. Jo Barraket, the study in 2010 assessed the landscape of the sector in Australia and estimated 20,000 social enterprises, a growth of nearly 40% over the past five years.[162] In the 2015 edition of the survey, challenges and opportunities in the space are outlined. These include reaching untapped marketplaces for social enterprises to sell and deliver products and services, financing and funding social enterprises, and finding the right staff and board members who share the social enterprise's view on pursuing mission and value.[163]

New Zealand's social enterprise sector has been developing rapidly over the last 5 years, with a broad range of ventures across a wide spectrum from trading NGOs to social mission-driven for-profit businesses. There is now a variety of infrastructure for people wanting to develop social enterprises—from incubator services, to accelerator programs, conferences, meetups, university courses and awards. The main players in this space include Akina Foundation, Inspiring Stories Trust, Enspiral, and Lifehack. Notably, there is still a gap in early stage funding for social impact focused ventures, and the traditional economic development infrastructure is slow to support the growing array of individuals and organisations who are looking to develop social enterprises.

A few verticals starting to emerge around the country which show a social enterprise space maturing include food, energy, environmental restoration, democracy, and well-being.

Legal structures haven't had a huge amount of attention, as New Zealand's existing structures are relatively easy to work

162 Australian Social Enterprise Facts. (n.d.). Retrieved from http://www.socialtraders.com.au/learn/dsp-default.cfm?loadref=209
163 Finding Australia's Social Enterprise Sector. (2015). Retrieved from http://www.socialtraders.com.au/what-we-do/dsp-default.cfm?loadref=426

with; however, B Corporation is working in the area to establish their structure and brand presence.[164] The country will also host the Social Enterprise World Forum for the first time, in 2017.[165]

44 HOW IS SOCIAL ENTERPRISE HAPPENING IN AFRICA AND THE MIDDLE EAST?

In the **Middle East**, the period of revolutions and protests challenging then-existing local government rule was termed the "Arab Spring". These movements of protest and civil disobedience catalyzed awareness and consciousness of massive unmet social issues in the regions in need of solutions. Chief among these is youth unemployment. The region is marked by an unprecedented proportion of youth, with over 30% of the population being within the age range of 15-29 years of age. This "youth bulge" can create a pathway for scaling social enterprise in the region, and can also signify the challenges ahead for the sector in this region. Studies have shown a correlation between a disproportionately high population of youth and increased civil conflict.[166] In fact, the post-Arab Spring years in the region have been called the "Arab Winter" to signify the upheaval experienced. Civil, economic, and political unrest are not ideal conditions in which social enterprise can thrive, because without legal structures and stability, engaging in impact-driven work can be hard, and it can be even harder to obtain funding to continue. However, the critical mass of young people can also be a boon to social enterprise as talented, motivated, impact-driven leaders seek to create solutions as entrepreneurs and within existing infrastructure.[167]

164 Rye, S. (2015, September 8). Social Enterprise in New Zealand [Written interview].
165 http://akina.org.nz/news/new-zealand-to-host-social-enterprise-world-forum-in-2017/
166 Kingsley, P. (2014, March 19). Does a growing global youth population fuel political unrest? Retrieved from http://www.theguardian.com/world/2014/mar/19/growing-youth-population-fuel-political-unrest-middle-east-south-america
167 Middle East Youth. (2015, July 10). Retrieved from http://www.brookings.edu/research/topics/middle-east-youth

Egypt is one example of a country in the region that has seen a tremendous upward trend in social entrepreneurship over the past decade.[168] It does not have a legal definition for social enterprise, and most impact-driven entities opt for a nonprofit, non-governmental organization (NGO) form, of which Egypt has 45,000.[169] However, the existing lack of infrastructure has created challenges for existing nonprofit social enterprises to partner with for-profit efforts and to raise funds, scale, and grow. While there have been calls to introduce a new social enterprise legal structure in Egypt, changes in the existing laws could also assist in fostering partnerships and enabling social enterprises to emerge and scale.[170]

Comprised of over fifty countries with a collective population hovering over one billion, **Africa** has been a major center for social entrepreneurship. Practitioners there, and those arriving on its shores from around the globe, are deploying social innovation in areas such as mobile money, education, healthcare, and agriculture to create powerful impact. These innovations are meeting needs that are urgent and massive. An estimated one-third of Africans regularly struggle to find enough food, and over 60% of adults on the continent are illiterate.[171] With various countries in Africa facing a ballooning population of youth, job creation is also a key need.

Fortunately, there is also powerful support for social enterprise in Africa. A growing number of high-profile funding opportunities, fellowships, and awards for social entrepreneurs lend not only capital but the valuable recognition and validation to support growth of the sector. These include One Acre Fund, African Development Bank, SEED Africa, Mandela

168 Younis, A. (2015, March 2). The Rise of the Social Entrepreneurs Is Egypt's Silent Revolution. Retrieved from http://www.huffingtonpost.com/alyaa-a-younis/the-rise-of-the-social-en_b_6787054.html
169 http://madad.com.eg/en/
170 (2014, September 1). Issue 4 - AUC Business Review - Fall 2014. Retrieved from http://www.aucegypt.edu/Business/ABR/Documents/ABR%20-%20Issue%204%20-%20Responsible%20Business%20-%20Fall%202014.compressed.pdf (p.60-63)
171 Literacy and non-formal education. (n.d.). Retrieved from http://www.unesco.org/new/en/dakar/education/literacy/

Washington Fellowship, Ashoka Africa Programs, and World Economic Forum on Africa, among others.

Additionally, the pan-African concept of *ubuntu* has the potential to cultivate a culture and unique ecosystem of collaboration and impact. Ubuntu, a Zulu word from South Africa, loosely translates to "I am, because you are" and speaks to a core belief within various African cultures that humanity cannot exist in isolation, and that generosity and collaboration are key to survival and success.[172]

Kenya provides a fascinating profile of social enterprise in Africa. As a country, it has been one of the most hospitable to social entrepreneurs, with hubs like Nairobi offering vibrant startup ecosystems for impact ideas to take root and grow. Often compared to Silicon Valley,[173] Nairobi is a bustling city with universities offering top talent and expertise, an ease of conducting business in English (one of the national languages), co-working spaces for social entrepreneurs, and funding opportunities. In fact, an estimated $650 million was invested in social enterprises within a five-year period of 2010.[174] Kenya is also the home to *M-Pesa*, one of the often-cited cases of the breakthrough potential of mobile money to offer banking to the base of the pyramid. M-Pesa lets people pay for goods and services through SMS text-messaging using simple (non-"smart") phones. Since its launch as an initiative within Vodafone in 2007, it has grown to over 17 million users[175] and has now been introduced to South Africa, India, Afghanistan, and Eastern Europe.

The urgent needs in Kenya include pervasive poverty, where more than 45% of Kenyans live below the nation's poverty line, and issues related to a disproportionately young population,

172 DeLuca, L., & Nakato, B. (2015, February 2). Social Entrepreneurship in Africa: What works, what doesn't – and why. Retrieved from http://www.seechangemagazine.com/?p=2270

173 Kohli, T. (2015, February 21). Why Kenya, home to Africa's 'Silicon Valley', is set to be the continent's ultimate tech hub. *Mail & Guardian Africa*. Retrieved from http://mgafrica.com/article/2015-02-19-why-kenya-is-africas-tech-hub

174 Weise, K. (2014, December 29). The Do-Good Startups of Nairobi. *Bloomberg Business*. Retrieved from http://www.bloomberg.com/bw/articles/2014-12-29/the-do-good-startups-of-nairobi

175 http://www.safaricom.co.ke/mpesa_timeline/timeline.html

where over 60% of Kenyans are younger than 25 years old. There is not a dedicated legal structure for social enterprise in Kenya; so social enterprises must elect to either operate as a nonprofit or to adopt a traditional for-profit company structure to pursue profit and impact.[176]

Ghana is a country poised for massive growth in social enterprise. Though the sector is relatively small, the country's stabilized economy and transition of power to a democratic leader provide a political and economic landscape in which social entrepreneurship can thrive. Ghana is unique as the social enterprise sector there is comprised largely of entrepreneurs and innovators in the Ghanaian diaspora who return to their homeland to address prevailing social issues such as persistent poverty. In fact, returning Ghanaians may be powering up to 60% of social enterprise activity there.[177] The country does not have a dedicated legal structure for social enterprise, but for-profit and nonprofit forms are both common.[178]

Where Ghana is in a period of stability and economic growth, **South Africa** is also growing as a center for entrepreneurship in consideration of its history of political divide, apartheid, and economic instability.[179] Still, remnants of the past remain as education, income inequality, and unemployment serve as major concerns for the nation. More South Africans collect state benefits than are employed, and nearly 80% of taxpayers below the tax threshold pay nothing in taxes.[180] The pressing needs have also served as a call to action for both international social innovators and, more recently, local entrepreneurs.

Renowned social innovation organization Ashoka has had

176 The Landscape for Impact Investing in East Africa. (2015, August 1). Retrieved from http://www.thegiin.org/knowledge/publication/the-landscape-for-impact-investing-in-east-africa
177 Darko, E. (2015, April 21). In Ghana, the Diaspora is Fueling a Social Enterprise Liftoff. Retrieved from http://nextbillion.net/blogpost.aspx?blogid=5397
178 Darko, E., & Korateng, K. (2015, March 1). Social Enterprise Landscape in Ghana. Retrieved from http://www.britishcouncil.org/sites/default/files/social_enterprise_landscape_in_ghana_report_final.pdf
179 Gumede, P. (2015, October 1). Social Enterprise in South Africa [Email interview].
180 Sloan, A. (2013, February 15). How social entrepreneurs are inspiring change across Africa. The Guardian. Retrieved from http://www.theguardian.com/social-enterprise-network/2013/feb/15/social-entrepreneurship-inspiring-change-africa

one of its longest-running programs in the region, with over 130 Fellows working in South Africa and surrounding countries.[181] The South African government's goal of eliminating poverty and reducing inequality by 2030 is a mandate for the country's growing social sector, comprised of an estimated 200,000 NGOs and numerous for-profit impact-focused ventures.[182] Though there is not a legal definition of social enterprise in South Africa, many social entrepreneurs opt for traditional for-profit or nonprofit structures, or a combination of the two.

In South Africa there are also growing legal obligations for corporations to engage in CSR and corporate social investment (CSI).[183] Stemming from the Amended Companies Act and the Bill of Rights of the country's Constitution, there is a call for companies to track impact, invest in social innovation, and engage social and ethics committees.[184] This trend along with the post-apartheid Black Economic Empowerment (BEE) initiative, have served to promote social impact and entrepreneurship by redistributing wealth and giving new entrepreneurs access to resources and opportunities to support success.

Also, there are a growing number of resources including centers, publications, awards and recognitions, and incubators and accelerators emerging to support the sector in South Africa. Examples of this developing social innovation ecosystem in the country include the Bertha African Enterprise Fund, Bertha Centre for Social Innovation and Entrepreneurship, The Social Investor Magazine, World Economic Forum on Africa, Ernst and Young Foundation South Africa, and SEED South Africa among others.

181 https://ashoka.org/regions/africa
182 Machi, N. (2015, March 26). 5 Great Opportunities in South Africa's Social Sector. Retrieved from http://emzingo.com/5-opportunities-in-south-africas-social-sector/
183 Flores-Araoz, M. (2011, September 2). Corporate Social Responsibility in South Africa: More than a nice intention. Retrieved from http://www.consultancyafrica.com/index.php?option=com_content&view=article&id=835:corporate-social-responsibility-in-south-africa-more-than-a-nice-intention&catid=82:african-industry-a-business&Itemid=266
184 Kirby, N. (2014, February). What's really right? Corporate Social Responsibility as a legal obligation in South Africa. Retrieved from http://www.werksmans.com/wp-content/uploads/2014/02/040233-WERKSMANS-feb-social-respons.pdf

45 IN WHAT NOTABLE WAYS IS SOCIAL ENTERPRISE UNFOLDING IN NORTH AND SOUTH AMERICA?

In **North America** beyond the U.S., Canada and Mexico are also showing some major developments.

In **Canada**, a few interesting initiatives and efforts have been introduced to support the growth of the social enterprise sector. In fact, in 2014, job growth in Canada's clean energy sector led the way among other sectors in the nation.

On Canada's west coast, **British Columbia** is the only province to introduce a new legal structure for social enterprise. Fashioned after the UK's Community Interest Corporation (CIC), British Columbia's Community Contribution Company (C3) came into effect in July, 2013.[185] The notable distinction between a C3 (and UK's CIC) and a traditional corporation is the idea of an "asset lock" — i.e., a cap on dividends owed to shareholders and distribution to shareholders in case of dissolution.[186] As of late 2015, over 30 companies in British Columbia have registered as C3s. Though British Columbia is the only province to pass the legislation, a "workaround" was implemented by the Social Enterprise Institute in Nova Scotia, which involves incorporating as a C3 in British Columbia and then registering "extra-provincially" in any province of the company's choosing.[187] Finally, and with regards to tax benefits, the Canada Regulatory Agency determined that C3s are not eligible for tax exemption, despite a charitable purpose.[188] In addition to leading the way with a legal structure, in 2015, British

---

185 http://www.centreforsocialenterprise.com/wp-content/uploads/2015/08/Structure_Shop_PPT.pdf
186 http://www.fin.gov.bc.ca/prs/ccc/caq.htm
187 Hybrid Social Enterprise: BC's Community Contribution Company, C3, Corporate Option is Available Across Canada! (2015, July 16). Retrieved from http://asiccc.ca/hybrid-social-enterprise-bcs-community-contribution-company-c3-corporate-option-available-across-canada/
188 Robertson, K. (2015, February 3). CRA letter on Community Contribution Companies distributing profits to a charitable organization. Retrieved from http://www.globalphilanthropy.ca/blog/cra_letter_on_community_contribution_companies_distributing_profits_to_a_ch

Columbia recognized May as "Social Enterprise Month" with programming and events centered around bringing awareness and drawing attention to the growing sector.

In western province **Alberta**, a massive 2014 initiative called the Social Innovation Endowment, which created a $1 billion fund for social innovation, was passed in March[189] and then cancelled in December after the province's then-Premier became entangled in controversies that ultimately led to her resignation.[190] The funds would have been allocated to research, design, and testing, and for the exploration and potential implementation of social impact bonds (i.e., a "pay for success" model in which the government pays a private company if they achieve a particular societal or social goal, as prescribed and mapped by a nonprofit in the space). The bill is currently tabled and being reviewed by the new administration, and other groups are exploring ways that Alberta can become a leader in social innovation.[191]

Mexico is increasingly becoming a major player in the world's economy. The World Bank predicts that Mexico will move from its current position as the 14th-largest economy to the sixth-largest world economy by 2050.[192] We, however, don't see that rate of growth translated to the country's social enterprise sector. In fact, social entrepreneurship is in its infancy in Mexico, with research indicating a count in the range of hundreds, no legal definition of social enterprise, and no sign of support for the sector in the country's business productivity and structural mapping detailed in the National Development

189 Ip, M. (2014, March 6). Alberta moves ahead with a monster social innovation fund, critics voice concerns about SIBs. Retrieved from http://www.socialenterprisebuzz.com/2014/03/06/alberta-moves-ahead-with-a-monster-social-innovation-fund-critics-voice-concerns-about-sibs/
190 Hemminger, P. (2014, December 28). The Unnoticed Death of a Billion-Dollar Endowment. Retrieved from http://theconsumption.ca/2014/12/28/death-of-a-billion/
191 Strutzenberger, M. (2015, February 17). Can Alberta Become a Social Innovation Leader? Retrieved from http://newscoopyyc.coop/can-alberta-become-a-social-innovation-leader/
192 Salter, A. (2015, May 12). A perfect storm for social enterprise in Mexico? *The Guardian*. Retrieved from http://www.theguardian.com/british-council-partner-zone/2015/may/12/a-perfect-storm-for-social-enterprise-in-mexico

Plan (2013-2018).[193] However, with the broad-ranging economic success, the influx of motivated youth, an entrepreneurial mindset, and pressing and urgent problems facing the country, —the elements for viable social entrepreneurship seem to be in place.

Pressing issues in Mexico include a widening wealth gap, where an estimated 75% of the country's 120 million residents earn less than $3,000 per year. Widespread government corruption has not only made citizens distrustful of certain civil society initiatives, but also poses a challenge for the growth of the impact sector. So too do instability caused by reigning drug cartels and persistent crime.[194] We'll have to see if the country's army of entrepreneurs and small businesses—an estimated 15% of adults in Mexico operate their own businesses, higher than the rate in the U.S., the UK, or France[195]—can use business models to create meaningful, sustainable impact.

In **South America**, the scene for social enterprise looks a lot like what is happening in Mexico. There is ample potential, both in demand for innovative solutions to societal issues and supply of talented problem-solvers, and also a few of the parallel concerns of lack of defined legal structure and government support, government corruption, and safety and crime issues that can negatively impact the emergence and growth of social enterprise. More than 80 million Latin Americans live on $2.50 or less per day, and 40 million youth lack formal employment.[196]

Another issue that comes up repeatedly, related to the sector in Latin America, is the lack of financing and funding. This scarcity can handicap promising ventures from achieving a critical mass in terms of traction and can halt operations just as these

193 Salter, A. (2015, May 12). A perfect storm for social enterprise in Mexico? *The Guardian*. Retrieved from http://www.theguardian.com/british-council-partner-zone/2015/may/12/a-perfect-storm-for-social-enterprise-in-mexico
194 Andrade, N. (2015, March 19). Social Entrepreneurship in Mexico: Local Solutions to Global Problems. *Huffington Post*. Retrieved from http://www.huffingtonpost.com/nelly-andrade/social-entrepreneurship-i_4_b_6904230.html
195 Salter, A. (2015, May 12). A perfect storm for social enterprise in Mexico? *The Guardian*. Retrieved from http://www.theguardian.com/british-council-partner-zone/2015/may/12/a-perfect-storm-for-social-enterprise-in-mexico
196 Tocalli, C. (2014, December 11). Working from the Inside Out: IDB's inaugural conference on scaling corporate social enterprise explores building bridges.

enterprises attempt to "cross the chasm" to achieving greater scale. Institutions such as Ashoka have had a presence in Latin America since the 1980s, and various entities such as Acumen, and Village Capital have a presence in the region as well.[197]

Columbia has seen remarkable economic growth in the past decade. This potential coupled with the challenges faced in the country have attracted the likes of Acumen and Village Capital to take major roles in supporting social entrepreneurship there. In May, 2015 Acumen announced expansion into Latin America,[198] specifically citing the goal of deploying at least $8 million in about ten opportunities in Colombia and Peru over the next five years, focusing on agriculture, education, and energy investments.[199] Village Capital also announced that Colombia would be it's 10th country of operation, with plans of establishing a base in Bogota and supporting social entrepreneurs, especially those working in the education space.[200]

Brazil also poses an interesting case for social enterprise. The past decade has brought economic growth and important initiatives to reduce extreme poverty. However, it remains one of the most unequal economies in the world. Additionally, an estimated 73% of students will drop out of school and only one in five young people will attend university. Additionally, more than 60% of the country does not have ready access to banking services.[201] The growth of the economy has also resulted in growth of investors looking for a return on impact in addition to a return on investment. In fact, in a report by the Aspen

197 Martínez, S. (2015, September 17). Why Are Social Enterprises Important in Latin America? Retrieved from http://socialmissions.com/2015/09/social-enterprises-in-latin-america/
198 Acumen Launches to Tackle Poverty in Latin America. (2015, May 4). Retrieved from http://acumen.org/blog/acumen-launches-to-tackle-poverty-in-latin-america/
199 Anderson, S. (2015, May 26). Into Acumen's Latin American Expansion: Patient capital fund hopes to deploy $8 million in 10 enterprises in Colombia and Peru in five years. Retrieved from http://nextbillion.net/blogpost.aspx?blogid=5438
200 Qadree, N. (2015, September 14). Building An Education Entrepreneurship Ecosystem in Latin America. Retrieved from https://www.linkedin.com/pulse/building-education-entrepreneurship-ecosystem-latin-america-qadree
201 Mapping the Impact Investing Sector in Brazil. (2014, May 1). Retrieved from http://www.aspeninstitute.org/sites/default/files/content/upload/AF_summary_english_06_eqom.pdf

Institute, an estimated fifteen of these impact investors entered the market in 2012 and, collectively, fund managers across various impact funds target raising over $150 million by the end of 2015, in a single year—a stark comparison to the $177 million raised for impact entrepreneurship in the past ten years.

> *Jay:* Thank you, Professor Zi. That is all very helpful to know! It will be great to meet entrepreneurs from some of these regions and be able to have some lens or context on their local ecosystems for social impact.

> *Professor Zi:* My pleasure, Jay. Please keep me posted on your social venture and trip to Malaysia. I may be in Thailand around that time.

CHAPTER 8

Social Entrepreneurs Q&A

ONE YEAR LATER

A YEAR PASSES, and the social enterprise has undergone some major changes.

The trip to Kuala Lumpur was eye-opening for the team. Through structured workshops, unstructured breakout sessions, and many group activities they had a chance to not only learn from social innovators across borders, but also interact and engage in meaningful ways. In fact, in one of the unconference sessions, a social enterprise working on nutrition issues in El Salvador suggested all food-related startups meet in one of the large conference rooms. Twelve startup teams, including *FreshDashDeliver*, joined the session, and they had a deep discussion about food deserts, how agriculture exports impact local communities, government regulations around community gardens, and selling home or community-grown food. There was not only a rich exchange of experience and thought leadership, but immense benefit also came through considering ways to collaborate internationally. The food sub-group created an email listserv which they still use to update each other and stay connected on ways to support, promote, and further good nutrition initiatives globally.

Within the company, there have also been some major shifts and iterations.

After defining target markets, *FreshDashDeliver* pivoted from the model of only door-to-door delivery of fresh food via delivery trucks to the addition of "pop-up" stalls where members of a community can come to purchase food or pick up orders. This move has centralized operations quite a bit and also streamlines transportation costs. They select locations near major public transportation hubs and have noticed that demand is greater because neighbors can just stop in when they have time in the day, rather than waiting for a delivery at a specific time.

More than anything, Sara, Jay, and Tino have been driven by the impact they have been seeing. In the neighborhoods where they increased access to fresh, healthy, affordable food, they have been tracking a trend of increased school attendance and decreased school dropout rates from the previous two years. One neighborhood was even inspired to start a community garden, while another saw a dip in neighborhood crime (though there isn't enough data to conclusively link the decrease to the access to healthy food). However, they have taken the advice to track impact early and consistently to heart. They are also tracking a few additional data points related to health, including obesity and heart disease, but any correlations there may not be clear for some time.

With the impact benchmarks, steady and increasing revenue, and significant new funding from a major foundation and cities grant, Sara, Jay, and Tino are now regularly approached regarding questions about social enterprise. From being new learners in the space, they are considered social entrepreneurs with promising early traction and deepening experience in the field.

At a conference for social enterprises promoting food security and sustainability, all three founders speak on a panel session titled "Founder Stories" and answer questions from the audience.

Woman from the audience: I have a question for Tino...

46 DO A LOT SOCIAL ENTERPRISES FAIL— HOW DO YOU OVERCOME FAILURE?

Oh sure they do. We got our start at a hackathon in San Francisco a year ago. Do you know how many companies from there are still working on their ideas? Less than thirty percent.

That's pretty consistent with what you see across the board for social enterprises. Serving different masters—the profit gods and the impact ones—can have its challenges.

But I'll share a trick that has helped us. We keep a small frame on our workstation that says "Have you failed enough today?" When we have our team meetings, we go around and talk about the ways we succeeded and failed. We make failure—which is a terrible word for experience—an integral and important part of our company. In that way, we can really learn from it and not only fail faster, but fail a little better. By that I mean, once we see that something is not working, we try to quickly quantify it so we understand what part didn't work.

From putting some numbers around both our successes and so-called failures and building grit, we then work as a team to make a story about the success or failure using the data. If we can prove that it's not a winning strategy, we let go of it and move the heck on. Instead of getting emotionally married to a certain way of doing things, we aim to make many mistakes, but quickly, and then pivot based on what we learn.

I also believe that it's not the failure that's critical, it's what happens after you fail, face setbacks, or experience challenges outside of your control. Some call it grit[202]—and we think it's

---

202 http://www.innov8social.com/2015/10/grit-the-super-power-for-entrepreneurs

the super power or 'secret sauce' to becoming a successful social entrepreneur.

The same woman from the audience: One more question for Tino...

47 HOW WAS THIS SOCIAL ENTERPRISE STARTUP EXPERIENCE COMPARED TO THE NUMEROUS OTHER STARTUPS YOU CO-FOUNDED?

It was very different from the past experiences that I had that were purely profit-driven. Thinking about impact creates both interesting and sometimes-challenging aspects related to accounting and figuring out ways to measure and improve the baselines. What's been great is that since social enterprise is becoming more of a known thing, there's often a unique camaraderie with our partners, funders, and beneficiaries. We've had the chance to inform and educate our funders and the communities that we serve about social entrepreneurship.

Man in the audience: I'd like to ask Jay a question...

48 WHAT HAVE YOU LEARNED ABOUT SOCIAL ENTERPRISE THAT YOU DIDN'T REALIZE BEFORE?

Even though so many states and jurisdictions have passed new legal structures for social enterprise, a lot of people still don't know that they exist, and though companies in each state have stepped up to be early adopters, what I have learned is that we are still in the early stages of wider adoption.

Companies are still learning and getting to know about the options available to them. What's really interesting to me as a law student is that these structures haven't been tested yet, and we don't know how they will hold up in court. The story is definitely still evolving, and we're still in the beginning chapters, at least in the U.S. It's been really fascinating to learn about how the legal structures have been evolving globally as well, and how a lot of countries with very successful entrepreneurs don't have these types of legal structures.

Young woman in the audience: Sara, you mentioned that you were originally interested in disrupting the access to healthy, affordable food—and your company is doing it...

49 WHAT OTHER AREAS EXCITE YOU FOR POTENTIAL DISRUPTION TO CREATE SOCIAL IMPACT?

Thanks for your question! It's been so cool to see how we have been able to disrupt the ways in which food can be served in local communities. It has definitely made me think about other areas ripe for social innovation. For example, the amazing innovations in Africa involving mobile technology that allows folks to pay for everything from groceries to healthcare has changed the game for access and mobility for the process of making and receiving payments. I have been starting to talk to startup entrepreneurs to better understand how we can use mobile money here in the U.S. to improve access to really important things and services, especially for people below the poverty line.

Another area in the space related to money that is really interesting is virtual currency, such as Bitcoin. It can allow for ease in transaction and openness between countries and areas with different monetary currencies. Virtual currencies create a unique possibility to fund social enterprise and removes friction in transferring and receiving payment overseas.

In areas of really cool tech such as drones and robotics, there has been incredible advancement in the past few years—with more applications, software, and possibilities. Deploying these technologies for tasks ranging from more accurately measuring impact to reaching individuals in remote regions definitely intrigues me too.

Also, from everything that I have seen, another area for disruption is education as we know it—both at the K-12 level as well as higher education. We have learned so much more about the process of learning and, through technology, have been able to find new ways to measure student learning and content retention—that we can see that if we want more people to sail, we need to build a better boat. And, we have the means to make that happen.

An older gentleman in the audience: A question for all of you...

50 WHAT HAVE BEEN THE GREATEST CHALLENGES IN STARTING A SOCIAL ENTERPRISE?

Tino: I guess I'm the old man here, so I'll go first. I've started a lot of businesses and had lots of successes as well as failures. What has been really challenging with the social enterprise is that you have to do everything to create a successful business but also to create positive social impact. We are always thinking about the impact we are creating, and we have pivoted many times when we realized that we weren't creating the impact we wanted. On all fronts, it has made a lot of sense all around. We've never had to compromise impact for profit; we have just had to be more creative to try to figure out how to achieve both.

Jay: That's all really true, Tino. I can jump in next. First of all, it's been really challenging going through law school and also being an entrepreneur. I wouldn't recommend it!

It's been interesting to see how the theory of law actually fits into practice of being an entrepreneur and starting a social enterprise. A lot of things that looked good on paper can be more challenging when you try to implement them, such as studying legal structures and then deciding on one. We realized it was a risk to take on a new one that has not been tested—but that we wanted to take that risk. We have also had to decide between different types of certifications too. We have learned to do our research, and then to just be ready to go on the journey from there.

Sara: Yes, and Jay is going to be really happy when he doesn't have to juggle both of his hats at the same time! For me, I am really glad I took this time after my associate's degree to be an entrepreneur. I was so passionate about serving my community. There's nothing I would rather have done during my gap year than start a business in this space. The biggest challenge for me is that, because I don't have as much formal education and experience in the industry, I have had to take more time to learn all the new terms and the mechanics of the business. This was challenging at times. It just takes time to learn how to navigate so many new things at once.

The panel moderator: A final question for all co-founders...

51　WHAT INSPIRES YOU TO PERSEVERE?

Sara: I'm going to jump in, guys.

For me, it was the very first time that we actually delivered our food. It was when we met individuals like Yolanda and her neighbors and knew that they don't have easy ways to get fresh produce, and that what we were doing was literally solving that problem—a light bulb went off. We can each do that in some way—we can be problem solvers.

It's those *real, raw* stories and the people we meet and connect with that make me feel so motivated. They have made me feel so sure about my decision to embark on this journey of social entrepreneurship and creating change in everything that we do.

Jay: Well, I'm in a really unique position because in the middle of my time in law school, I also have been lucky enough to have this experience. It's made me really driven to become an attorney to help entrepreneurs, and to help them to launch businesses that will create positive change.

I think what makes me persevere is the fact that I can literally apply everything we've gone through and use it all to be a better lawyer and serve the new kinds of startups that are emerging. I hope that I can share my experience, both as an entrepreneur and with my knowledge in law, in the future—in whatever I do.

Tino: I hope I can finally retire! I already came out of retirement to start this business, but I'm afraid I'm a little hooked now.

I already had a long career in investing, and when I did my Peace Corps mission in Botswana, I saw a whole different world and a whole different set of unmet needs. Being able to create a business that could address both kinds of things has been really empowering.

I'd like to be able to tell my friends who have even more grey hair than me, about the options we have today to create social ventures. Maybe some of the men and women that I know might be funding some of these new social enterprises.

Going from being in a traditional business and investing to starting something like this has given me a new perspective on launching, funding, and scaling a social enterprise. I think that people who are more experienced can really step up to advise and mentor and provide the funding that is so critical to social entrepreneurs who are just starting out.

* * *

Sara, Jay, and Tino take the train back to the IMPACTATHON offices in silence. The experience of speaking on the panel was invigorating and they are each lost in reflection of the past year and the work ahead. A few interesting things came out of the conference session. One was that a few students approach the co-founders after the talk to find out how they could apply to intern, work, or be a fellow at *FreshDashDeliver*. On the spot, they each recommended sending resumes, samples of work, and LinkedIn profiles to the company email address. During the coffee break after, the three did a quick huddle and decided they should definitely create opportunities for other aspiring social entrepreneurs to gain experience.

But that wasn't what had each of them deep in thought now. Just as they were exiting the conference, they had the surreal and amazing experience of meeting Malala Yousafzai—youngest Nobel Peace Prize recipient, and someone who embodies the potential and possibility of generation Z and of social innovation. She was standing under a banner featuring one of her quotes, "I raise up my voice-not so I can shout but so that those without a voice can be heard." They approached her and spoke to her for just moments and explained their work. She smiled and handed them a small mail-in postcard addressed, and stamped to her foundation's headquarters which contained a single question in small typeface amid blank space, and which they now pondered.

How are you a voice for the unheard?

Acknowledgements

THIS BOOK HAS BEEN A JOURNEY, a process, a challenge, and an incredible joy and privilege to work on. I am deeply grateful for the good energy of so many to make this happen. Some part of my life's purpose is entwined with my work on Innov8social.com and its extensions such as this book. I hope in some small way to invite individuals into the space of social entrepreneurship and inform and encourage exploration of our powerful potential to create social impact in innovative ways.

In no particular order, and with good energy all around, I want to thank my mom Punita for living life so boldly and fully, my dad Dipak for believing we can achieve literally anything, my sister Sejal for being a constant source of inspiration in the undefined spaces of entrepreneurship and life, my nephew Sukhman, my brother Sunil, sister-in-law Neetu, and Nani for providing encouragement and levity throughout the past few years of this project. And thank you to pup Bella for your love, companionship, and taking me out for regular walks during the writing and editing process.

Thank you to the editors, reviewers, and collaborators who have helped bring this book to life, and given it wings. Beth, Sasha, Karin, Carly, Matt, Noah, Kate, Sue, Julie, Parimala, Karthik, Mary, Myles, Varun, Dominika, Rah, Puja, Joe, Shannon, Barb, Diane, Lisset, Edward, Jerry, Preeti, Avni, Tom, Mary Lea, Archana, Quyhnchi, Sean, Philile, Adam, Erik, Sam,

Unmesh, Resh, Nidhi, Geeta, David, Devang, Ketie, Steph, Amisha, Sean, Pradeep, Aidan, Somya, Melinda, Andrew, Heather, Nikhil, John.

Thank you to the supporters and encouragers who believed from the very start: Emily, Mike, Erin, Chitrak, Frank, Henry, Illa, Raju, Siddharth, Adithi, Sydney, Komnieve, Karthik, Renika, Maya, Prasanna, Sukanya, Sayee, Komal, Parshad, Rakhee, Anika, Ashna, Annu, Preeti, Keshav, Arjun, Hiral, Shailo, Sonali, Mukesh, Nina, Nirja, Xavier, Poonam, Inder, Armaan, Neha, Dennis, Christine, Mathew, Jordan, Niyati, Mitul, Karen, Alexandra, Rahul, Sonali, Reshma, Shamil, Naya, Kalen, Luke, Urvi, Kiren, Nitin, Michael, Siejen, Pete, Jenny, Stephanie, Ajita, Munira, Moiz, Mohammed, Maryam, Shefali, Amish, Sonam, Avni, Sonal, Atur, Roshan, Maggie, Graham, Hallie, Andy, Amy, Rupal, Aneil, Shailen, Sienna, Samir, David, Aimee, Hannah, Daniel, Janelle, Jasmeen, Ammu, Tom, Rabeeza, Leonard, Zeke, Savi, Armaan, Sameer, Payal, Aarav, Renu, Sachin, Ayan, Aniketa, Natalia, Krishna, Andrew, Semyon, Erik, Rohini, Vasu, Saanvi, Ishaan, Yacanex, Enisha, Sanah, Sajid, Sara, Chet, Nidhi, Zoe, Andy, Yvette, Mike, Satish, Neetu, Sachin, Akash, Nitin, Joel, Venu, Gita, Sheetal, Avi, Emmie, Nick, Sean, Unmesh, Hetal, Sachin, Kanan, Darsh, Rajat, Carm, Bharat, Ruki, Gouri, Milap, Mehaan, Harsha, Sameer, Kamila, Natasha, Phil, Natasha, Bela, Mahesh, Neha, Nisha, Rajan, Gautami, Walifai, Seth, Meena, Madhu, Pragna and all of the family and friends around the globe whose good energy has been part of this journey.

About the Author

NEETAL PAREKH is an attorney by education, a digital content strategist by training, and a social innovator and storyteller at heart. She specializes in social enterprise business models and legal structures, startup methodologies, social media strategy, writing/blogging, and public speaking. Neetal is the Founder and CEO of Innov8social, which builds tools to help individuals and companies reach their impact potential. She is the host of the Innov8social Podcast, featuring interviews with thinkers and doers in the social impact space. She loves sharing ideas and knowledge through mentorship, coaching, public speaking and blogging. Neetal serves as an advisor and mentor to social enterprise startups and has been selected as a 2016 Starting Bloc Fellow.

She also admittedly finds a certain thrill composing just the right content for just the right platform. Offline, you can find Neetal taking walks with dog, Bella, listening to audiobooks, or spending time with family and friends. Online, you can find her on social media at @neetalparekh and @innov8social, likely using one of her favorite hashtags—#goanddo!

CPSIA information can be obtained
at www.ICGtesting.com
Printed in the USA
LVOW03s1606230118
563697LV00014B/1418/P